1812:

The War for Canada

A Year With A War Named After It

A humorous look at the War of 1812. A short, somewhat unknown war, fought in small, somewhat unknown places. Other than Detroit, Toronto, Niagara Falls, Buffalo, Washington, Baltimore and New Orleans, The War of 1812 was fought in small places that are still somewhat small and unknown today. A war fought in small places it might have been. But it was a war fought for a big continent.

"SOME DISHCLOTHS PICKUP THE WATER, AND SOME JUST PUSH IT AROUND."

- MY MOTHER

The Publisher: DESPUB

2340B Clifton Street, Allanburg, Ontario, Canada L0S 1A0

Library and Archives Canada Cataloguing in Publication

Corfield, Geoffrey, 1949-
1812 : a year with a war named after it / Geoffrey Corfield
Includes index.

ISBN 978-0-9865370-4-2

    1. Canada -- History -- War of 1812. I. Title
    FC442.C6752012   971.03'4   C2011-9068669-9

Editing / design:	David E. Scott
Cover Illustrations:	Jenniffer Julich, Jnnffr Productions, www.jnnffr.com
Illustrations:	Inkblot Geoffrey Corfield
Printing:	AGMV Marquis / Québec

Published without financial assistance from any agency of the federal or provincial governments.

A DESPUB PUBLICATION

Table of Contents

CHAPTER ONE

Introduction:

Before the War of 1812

The War of 1812 officially started on 18 June 1812. In the afternoon. It lasted two years, six months and six days, and ended in the early evening. Because of this it's sometimes known as The War of 1812-14. But mostly it's just known as The War of 1812.

The year of 1812 has an overture named after it as well. "*The 1812 Overture*" by Tchaikovsky was named after another war that was going on in 1812. A bigger, longer, much better-known war. The Napoleonic Wars in Europe lasted from 1793 until 1815. The War of 1812 in North America started while this war was going on, and ended just before this war ended. But of course nobody at the time knew just when these two wars were going to end, or even if they would end.

The sort of cannon used by the percussion section of The Berlin Philharmonic Orchestra for their 1967 rendition of "The 1812 Overture" by Tchaikovsky.

The war in Europe affected The War of 1812 in North America. But The War of 1812 in North America had little effect on the war in Europe. In fact most of Europe didn't even know The War of 1812 existed. And still don't.

The War of 1812 really only involved two countries and one future country. The two countries were Great Britain, then also fighting France and Napoleon in the other war in Europe; and The United States of America, then an independent country for 36 years and fighting Britain again 29 years after the end of The American Revolutionary War. The one future country was Canada, then six separate colonies of Britain and not to be an independent country itself for another 55 years. The War of 1812's importance to these three countries however is quite different.

To Great Britain The War of 1812 is not important and never has been. It was an unwanted distraction to the much more important war going on in Europe against Napoleon, and is hardly ever remembered in Britain today, if at all.

To The United States of America though The War of 1812 is actually more important than it's made out to be, trailing as it does in popularity and importance behind The American Civil War (most popular), and The American Revolutionary War (most important). The War of 1812 paved the way for The United States to expand south to Florida and west of the Mississippi, even if it couldn't expand north to Canada. It eventually gave The United States the states of Maine and Washington as they exist today. And it provided The United States with four future war-hero presidents: Monroe, Adams, Jackson, Harrison; a national anthem; a famous White House; four famous sayings: "Don't Give Up The Ship," "We Have Met The Enemy And They Are Ours," "Remember The River Raisin," and "Uncle Sam;" a uniform colour: "West Point Grey;" and a regimental motto: "I'll try, Sir" (21st Infantry Regiment).

To Canada however, The War of 1812 meant the most. To Canada The War of 1812 meant that 53 years later there would be a chance for a country called Canada to exist. For if The United States had won The War of 1812, which it fully intended to do, then there would either not be a country called Canada today, or it would be a considerably smaller Canada than it is now. In fact, as things turned out, as a result of The War of 1812 Canada was actually unlucky not to end up bigger than it is today (it could have had northern Maine and Washington state).

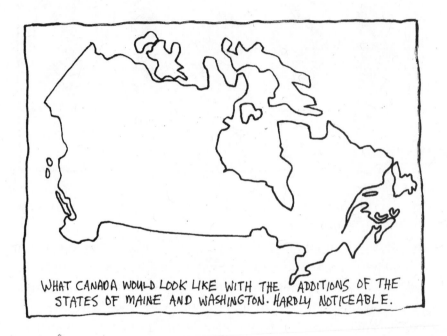

WHAT CANADA WOULD LOOK LIKE WITH THE ADDITIONS OF THE STATES OF MAINE AND WASHINGTON. HARDLY NOTICEABLE.

One of the reasons The War of 1812 is not better known is that it was not a particularly good war at producing heroes. There aren't many of them. Indeed there are several civilians whose part in the war is remembered as much or more than the few military participants who distinguished themselves.

For the British, their most famous general in the war is Major-General Sir Isaac Brock, who is responsible for the early British victories in the war, but dies gloriously in battle when the war is only four months old, and actually becomes more of a Canadian hero than a British hero.

Lieutenant-General Sir George Prevost is in charge of the entire defence of Canada, and does a good job of it, but then goes and loses The Battle of Plattsburgh towards the end of the war, dies shortly after the war ends, and does not become a hero.

General Brock   Isaac Chauncey   Oliver Hazard Perry   Laura Secord   Tecumseh

SOME HEROES OF THE WAR OF 1812
(shown in silhouette in an oval frame)

For the Americans, Commodore Oliver Hazard Perry sews the words "Don't Give Up The Ship" in white letters on a blue flag, then proceeds to give up the ship, but takes his flag along with him to another ship, doesn't give that ship up, and wins a naval battle on Lake Erie that in the end doesn't really amount to much, but results in him sending back the triumphant message "We Have Met The Enemy And They Are Ours," thus making sure that everybody remembers it and he becomes a hero.

General Andrew Jackson organizes the successful defence of New Orleans when the war is unofficially over but both sides don't know it yet, becomes a hero, and then goes on to become President of The United States.

Francis Scott Key, a lawyer, writes a poem that eventually becomes the American national anthem; and Samuel Wilson, although not famous as Samuel Wilson, becomes famous as "Uncle Sam," the American army meat inspector whose stamping of army meat "U.S." becomes known as the stamp of The United States government and its official nickname.

For the Canadians, other than General Brock, two other non-military people become Canadian heroes. Tecumseh, the Indian leader who organizes the Indian's support of the British and dies gloriously in battle; and Mrs. Laura Secord, who walks 19 miles to warn the British of an American attack leading to the British ambushing the Americans at "The Battle of Beaver Dams." And that, give or take the odd local hero here and there, is about it as far as heroes go for The War of 1812. Not a lot.

But trying to follow a war by its generals, commanders, personalities and heroes involved is confusing. You forget who's on who's side. So in this book, except for particular circumstances, the two sides will just be identified as American and British.

There were also British who fought with the Americans, Indians who fought with the Americans, and Canadians who fought with the Americans; and Americans who fought with the British, Indians who fought with the British, and Canadians who fought with the British. But unlike The American Revolutionary War there were no French or Germans involved. The War of 1812 was a strictly English-speaking war (with Indian interpreters).

Like all wars The War of 1812 started because somebody didn't like somebody else. In this case because The United States of America didn't like Great Britain. They didn't like Britain's navy stopping their ships from trading with Europe. They didn't like Britain's navy stopping their ships to "impress" American sailors into the Royal Navy. And they also didn't like Britain supporting the Indians against them in the "west" (Ohio, Michigan, Indiana, Illinois, Wisconsin).

The United States didn't like these things so it decided to declare war on Britain. Officially. Having declared war on Britain it then decided to invade and conquer Britain. Not the Britain part of Britain, just the North American part of Britain. Canada. The United States would invade and conquer Canada and take it from Britain, that's all. Shouldn't be such a difficult thing to do should it? Britain wouldn't put up much of a fight because they were already fighting

France in Europe. And the Canadians wouldn't put up much of a fight because there were lots of Americans in Canada already and they would welcome more of them. All they had to do really was just walk in and take over.

The United States had actually wanted to take Canada from Britain even before it became The United States. In 1775, right at the start of The American Revolutionary War, the Americans attacked Montreal and Quebec City, Canada. They failed to get them, but it was a pretty daring (and foolhardy) attack. George Washington also had plans for invading Canada in 1778, 1780 and 1781 that were never tried (the French wouldn't help them). At the end of The American Revolutionary War the American peace negotiators, including Benjamin Franklin, thought that the annexation of Canada might be something that they could talk about. So the idea of invading and conquering Canada was definitely something that The United States had had in mind for quite some time prior to 1812 (37 years).

The War of 1812 was a war of skirmishes and small battles rather than big battles. A war fought as much from behind trees as in formation. More people were killed in one battle in Europe than participated in the whole of The War of 1812 in North America (at The Battle of Leipzig in October 1813 the French alone lost 68,000). Yet the stakes were just as high. At stake was the fate of a continent. A continent nobody at the time knew just how big it was (it was 2.3 times bigger than Europe).

If Napoleon had won then perhaps more of Europe would now be French. But if The United States had won then undoubtedly more of North America would now be American. That it isn't is the story of The War of 1812. How there came to be two countries north of Mexico, not just one.

CHAPTER TWO

The Start of the War of 1812

There are six things to remember about The War of 1812: What went on before the war, who started the war, the two sides involved in the war, geography, water, and the weather.

Before 1812 there were a number of events that occurred that eventually led to The United States of America declaring war on Great Britain. During the American Revolutionary War (1775-1783), the Americans attack Montreal and Quebec City, Canada, lose (1775), but beat the British at The Battle of Saratoga, New York (1777). The significance of these two events is that a young American officer James Wilkinson is present at both battles, develops a particular enthusiasm for invading and conquering Canada, and in 1812 is now a high-ranking general in the American Army.

In 1794 the Americans defeat the Indians at The Battle of Fallen Timbers near Toledo, Ohio. The significance of this event is that an Indian chief named Tecumseh is present at the battle and develops a particular hatred for Americans. Also present are two American officers who by 1812 are now both high-ranking American generals, the same James Wilkinson already mentioned, and William Henry Harrison who Tecumseh especially doesn't like.

In 1803 France sells Louisiana to The United States for 80 million francs (1,675.32 francs per square mile for the present-day state of Louisiana, but which at the time of 1803 meant "all the land between the Mississippi River and the Rocky Mountains," considerable less francs per square mile than that). The significance of this event is that France now has more money to spend on the war in Europe. Britain doesn't like this as Britain is one of those countries fighting France in Europe (France also supported

The United States in The American Revolutionary War against Britain, which Britain didn't like either).

In 1806 Britain and France prohibit trade with each other by anybody else, including The United States. The United States doesn't like this. In 1807 The United States prohibits trade by itself with anybody else, including Britain and France (later amended in 1809 to prohibit trade with Britain and France only).

Also in 1807 the British ship *Leopard* stops the American ship *Chesapeake* and demands that it submit to a search for British deserters (some British sailors had skipped off into Hampton, Virginia). The *Chesapeake* refuses. The *Leopard* opens fire on the *Chesapeake* killing three. The *Chesapeake* surrenders and the British take four sailors off the *Chesapeake* and instantly enroll them in The Royal Navy. The United States doesn't like this.

Anatomy of a Tomahawk
Production Drawing
(courtesy: Tippecanoe Tomahawk
and Scalp Restoration Company,
Lafayette, Indiana)

In 1811 the British ship *Guerrière* takes one sailor off an American ship. The United States doesn't like this. The American ship *President* sails after the *Guerrière* and sinks another British ship the *Little Belt*. Britain doesn't like this.

The Royal Navy at this time has some 1,048 ships (minus the *Little Belt*), carrying 28,000 cannons and 158,000 sailors. It is estimated that since 1807 Britain had seized 389 American ships (France had seized 558), and between 1807-1812 taken 10,000 sailors off American ships, most of whom were genuine Americans and not British deserters seeking the bright lights of Hampton, Virginia. The United States doesn't like this.

Also in 1811 the Americans defeat the Indians at The Battle of Tippecanoe near Lafayette, Indiana. The significance of this event is that the American general present is William Henry Harrison again, the one that Tecumseh really doesn't like, and immediately after the battle Tecumseh takes his Indian Confederacy to Amherstburg, Ontario, Canada and pledges to fight with the British against the Americans and William Henry Harrison, who Tecumseh really, really doesn't like now. (When Harrison was later running for president his running mate was John Tyler, and their election slogan was "Tippecanoe and Tyler too.")

Also in 1811 a group of American politicians state that "The Greater Disposer of Human Events intended those two rivers (the Mississippi and the St. Lawrence), to belong to the same people", and that The United States "should stretch from Panama to Hudson Bay." Britain doesn't like this. The year of 1811 is an especially bad year for Britain. The French are winning in Europe; the Americans are saying bad things about them; and in Britain itself there are poor harvests, food shortages, unemployment and riots. And The War of 1812 is only one year away.

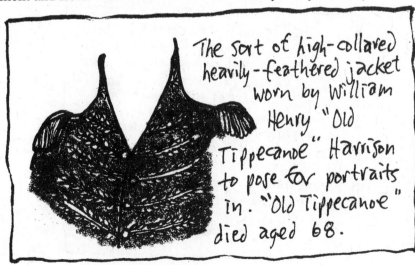

The sort of high-collared heavily-feathered jacket worn by William Henry "Old Tippecanoe" Harrison to pose for portraits in. "Old Tippecanoe" died aged 68.

"Peace as we have it, is disgraceful, and war is honourable."

One 1 June 1812 the American president James Madison recommends a declaration of war against Britain.

On 4 June 1812, the American House of Representatives passes a declaration of war against Britain by a vote of 79 to 49.

"I think the business way too hasty" (one of the 49).

On 17 June 1812, the American Senate passes the declaration of war against Britain by a vote of 19 to 13.

The states of Connecticut, Delaware and Rhode Island are strongly against the war. The states of Georgia, North Carolina, Pennsylvania, South Carolina, Tennessee, Vermont and Virginia are strongly for the war. The states of Massachusetts, New Jersey and New York are more against the war than for the war. The states of Kentucky, Maryland and New Hampshire are more for the war than against the war. Ohio is split. The end result is that The United States is more for the war than against it.

On 18 June 1812, the American president signs the war bill and The United States of America officially declares war on Great Britain.

The quill pen, inkwell and inkstand on desk covered with oversized, tumbling-down, dragging-on-floor, heavy-fringed tablecloth; arm with scroll motif of heavy wooden chair mostly obscured in shadow; and large book carelessly left on floor leaning up against desk and oversized tablecloth; in the famous 1810 engraving of James Madison during The War of 1812 by David Edwin.

"The free-born sons of America . . . to follow the Lord of Hosts . . . in a righteous cause . . . "

"I am not for stopping at Quebec or anywhere else. I would take the entire continent."

"In four weeks from the time that a declaration of war is heard on our frontiers, the whole of Upper Canada (Province of Ontario) and part of Lower Canada (Province of Quebec) will be in our possession."

"We will take Canada."

"The acquisition of Canada this year as far as the neighbourhood of Quebec, will be a mere matter of marching."

"The militia of Kentucky are alone competent to place Montreal and Upper Canada at your feet."

"We shall succeed in obtaining what it is important to obtain (Canada), and that we shall experience little annoyance or embarrassment in the effort."

"One-half of the militia of both provinces (Ontario and Quebec) would join our standard."

"The poor Canadians have been forced into this war."

In June 1812 Britain is still fighting France in Spain, and Napoleon is advancing into Russia.

The United States of America quite expected to win The War of 1812. Easily. A doddle. But talking about a war and declaring a war are two quite different things from actually fighting a war.

In the 29 years since the end of The American Revolutionary War the American Army hasn't done much except shrink. Its generals are old Revolutionary War veterans. They have no experienced military leaders, and, more importantly, no George Washington waiting in the wings in a blue uniform to come riding to the rescue on a white horse.

REGULATIONS
for the
Field Exercises, manoeuvres, and
conduct of the

INFANTRY
of The United States

Drawn up and adapted to
the Organization of the
MILITIA and
REGULAR TROOPS

Copied from the French 1792
manual by an Officer
of the Army by Order of the
SECRETARY OF WAR (please
don't tell Napolean)

With Explanatory Plates showing
soldiers in French uniforms
(we hardly have any uniforms)

PHILADELPHIA

City Tavern Printing Co. 1812

Title Page For The American
Army Regulations Manual
1812 (first draft)

In 1801 the American Army has 4,000 poorly paid, poorly equipped, and poorly trained soldiers still using the same army training manual written at Valley Forge (1778). Their uniforms are poor quality and are either black, brown, grey or blue depending upon which colour of cloth was on sale at the time (they also had a tendency to purposely have the jacket sleeves too long to allow for shrinkage).

By 1807 the American Army is down to 2,400 soldiers, but is now starting to re-equip itself. By 1812 with a population of 7.5 million and the potential to raise 35,000 regular soldiers and 100,000 militia; the American Army is up to 6,744 regular soldiers, 5,000 new recruits, 10 ships, 63 gunboats, 4,000 sailors, and 1,800 marines (soldiers on ships).

However as American government policy is to prefer part-time state militia soldiers to full-time federal regular soldiers, the United States orders the states to get their militias ready. Connecticut, Massachusetts, Rhode Island and Vermont refuse. Britain isn't going to attack them. Militias are only for defending their states with, not for invading and conquering Canada. Of the states that are in favour of the war, the Carolinas, have one gun for every two soldiers, Virginia one gun for every five soldiers, and Georgia even less than that (when they can find the gun).

There is even the idea that The United States won't even need soldiers to invade and conquer Canada with anyway. They can just send officers over the border who will organize the Canadians to fight against the British themselves. The United States is counting very much on the Canadians joining them in this war. They also think that since Britain is also at war with France, that once The United States has invaded Canada, Britain will quickly seek peace under American terms, and The United States will get Canada, or even part of Canada, without even fighting The War of 1812 at all. It doesn't quite work out like this (none of it does).

The Americans don't know it but the British are not prepared to give up Canada without a fight. They send what troops they can spare to North America, determine a war strategy based on defence, work with the Canadian militia to get them ready, and let them get on with it.

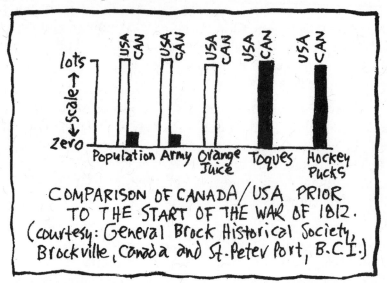

COMPARISON OF CANADA/USA PRIOR TO THE START OF THE WAR OF 1812. (courtesy: General Brock Historical Society, Brockville, Canada and St. Peter Port, B.C.I.)

In 1802 the British Army sends 33-year-old Brigadier-General Isaac Brock to Canada (Major-General in 1811). He doesn't want to go to Canada and he hates Canada when he gets there. He hates the climate and he hates being stuck out in the middle of nowhere when all the action is going on in Europe. But he gets on with it.

Brock visits Quebec City, Montreal, Toronto (Fort York), and Niagara-on-the-Lake (Fort George) 1802-05; he orders militias to train (six days a month); issues them with guns (one per soldier); puts them on stand-by (1808); and proposes that veteran British soldiers be posted to Canada (they are).

In 1812 Canada has a population of 300,000; 5,600 British regular soldiers spread over an area of 1,100 miles; 70,000 militia; 5,000 Indians; one Indian chief named Tecumseh who really hates Americans; and one major-general named Isaac Brock who really turns out to be quite good at his job.

The British have a small number of experienced regular soldiers (some of the best soldiers in the world at this time), some competent generals, a militia who they help to train, and Indians who are really good at surprise attacks and scaring the enemy (so terrified are the Americans of being scalped by Indians that they surrender a number of times during this war just to be kept away from them).

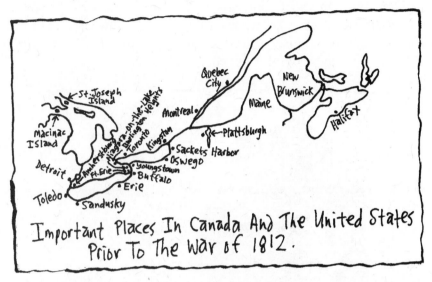

Important Places In Canada And The United States Prior To The War of 1812.

The Americans have a regular army that is small, untrained, unprepared and does not work with the militia; a militia that doesn't always cooperate with the regular army (several times during this war they refuse to invade and don't); generals that are inexperienced and incompetent; and a war strategy that is erratic, poorly organized and poorly executed. Unfortunately for the Americans as well, these things never really improve much as the war goes along. Yet The United States still has their chances to win. They still could have won this war, or at least gotten something out of it (besides a national anthem and a White House).

North America is a big place. With lots of geography (Canada and the USA together are 1.8 times bigger than Europe).

In 1812 Canada is a long, thin country strung out along the north shores of the St. Lawrence River, Lake Ontario and Lake

Erie in the provinces of Ontario and Quebec; with isolated pockets of settlement on the east coast (Nova Scotia, New Brunswick, Newfoundland). The more inland away from water you went, the more sparsely populated wilderness you got. The best road system is between Quebec City and Montreal. West of Montreal the road to Kingston, Ontario is only good in winter. West of Kingston you're on your own. To get from the western parts of Ontario to Montreal takes almost as long as to get from Quebec City to Britain. Canada is a wilderness country held together by water.

The sort of jacket with hanging ropes and lots of braiding preferred by Sir George Prevost, Governor General and Commander-in-Chief of Canada during The War of 1812.

The British send Lieutenant-General Sir George Prevost to Quebec City to command the defence of Canada (1811). The British war strategy is defence. The most important and strongest points are Halifax, Nova Scotia and Quebec City, Quebec. The rest of the country: Montreal, Quebec; and Kingston, Toronto, St. Joseph Island, Burlington, Amherstburg, Niagara-on-the-Lake, Chippawa and Fort Erie, Ontario; can all be lost and retaken, just so long as Halifax and Quebec City are held.

In 1812 The United States of America is still primarily an Atlantic seaboard country. The more inland away from the ocean you went, the more isolated and undeveloped you got. And this includes the states of Michigan and Vermont, and the northern parts of New York, Ohio and Pennsylvania. The states that border on Canada. The very states that you have to invade through in order to invade Canada. An area where roads are mainly clearings through woods, and where lake and river traffic are more important than roads. In order to invade the wilderness of Canada then, you first have to invade the wilderness of The United States. The War of 1812 is a war in the wilderness.

The American war strategy is offensive (it has to be, you can't invade and conquer without attacking). They will take Ontario and Quebec, then New Brunswick and Nova Scotia, but not Newfoundland (too far away). Halifax, Nova Scotia is the most important target since it is the North American base for The Royal Navy.

Then they have second thoughts. Quebec City and Halifax are too strong to attack, so they will take Montreal and everything west of Montreal including Kingston, Ontario. This will break the line of communication between Quebec City and the rest of Canada to the west, and give The United States most of Canada anyway. Invading, attacking and conquering Canada is more difficult in the east, and gets easier the further west you go. This is a good strategy and a better strategy than the first strategy, but unfortunately they don't stick to this strategy either.

The United States plans a four-pronged invasion of Canada: east from Detroit, Michigan to take Amherstburg, Ontario; west from Buffalo, New York to take the Niagara Peninsula of Ontario; north from Sackets Harbour, New York to take Kingston, Ontario; and north from Lake Champlain, New York to take Montreal, Quebec. The Americans begin assembling two armies at Albany, New York and Dayton Ohio. Two outposts in the wilderness.

Three of the American objectives are in Ontario. The British commander in Ontario province is Isaac Brock. He is ordered not to take offensive operations "except for the purpose of preventing or repelling Hostilities or unavoidable Emergencies," and that are "solely calculated to strengthen a defensive attitude."

Brock considers being invaded "Hostilities and Emergencies," and that attacking before being attacked can "strengthen a defensive attitude." So Brock forms an offensive-defensive strategy. The British will take Mackinac Island, Michigan and Detroit, Michigan from the Americans. This will secure for them the allegiance of Tecumseh and the Indians. He also considers that the Niagara Peninsula of Ontario will be the prime invasion target of the Americans. He guesses right on both counts (how did he know the Americans would not attack Kingston, Ontario and never will?).

North America is a big place. With lots of water. Some of the biggest freshwater lakes in the world are in North America. Lake Ontario, the smallest of the five Great Lakes, is just slightly smaller than Wales or the American state of New Jersey.

The Great Lakes form part of the Canada/USA border today as they did in 1812. In 1812 most of the border between Canada and The United States is water. Lakes and rivers. In order to invade during this war then, the invading side will have to cross water. This means that once they have invaded they will have the insecure feeling of being trapped in enemy territory with water between them and home. Both sides suffer from this sense of insecurity during the war, but it especially affects the Americans. They are after all the invading side in this war, and the one to whom success in this war depends upon invading.

The two sides crisscross the Canada-USA border many times during this war. This is not just a war about the Americans invading Canada as it started out to be. The British actually invade The United States more times than the Americans invade Canada. Although the main part of the war should have taken place in the Canadian provinces of Quebec and Ontario east of Kingston, and the American states of New York (northeastern part) and Vermont; it doesn't. The Americans don't stay true to their original invasion targets of Montreal and Kingston. They attack further west. So most of the war takes place in Ontario west of Kingston, and the states of New York (northwestern part), Ohio and Michigan instead.

The easiest stretches of water to get across are the rivers: the St. Lawrence River, the Niagara River, and the Detroit River. The Americans try major invasions across the St. Lawrence River once (but in an odd way), the Detroit River three times, and the Niagara River three times. The Americans will invade Canada 12 times during this war (not counting other smaller skirmishes and raids), but each time, except for once, they will get this insecure feeling and return to their side of the border without staying very long. The exception is Amherstburg, Ontario which the Americans take in late 1813 and have to give back at the end of the war. The American Army becomes an invading army that will just not stay invading.

The British will actually invade The United States 14 times themselves during this war (not counting other smaller skirmishes and raids), strictly as a "defensive attitude." But most of the time they too will get this insecure feeling and return to their side of the border without staying very long. The exceptions are Mackinac Island, Michigan; northern Maine; Fort Astoria, Oregon; Prairie du Chien, Wisconsin; and Fort Niagara (Youngstown), New York; all of which the British have to give back at the end of the war.

North America is a big place. With lots of weather. And in the part of the North American continent where The War of 1812 takes place, it's hot in summer and cold in winter. So if you're going to invade Canada your strategy should be to get going early in the spring, get your invading over and done with as soon as possible before fall, and get yourself entrenched in your newly-invaded territory before winter sets in. Then be ready to move again and do your conquering next spring.

Or, like the British did several times during this war, if you were prepared for it, you could invade in winter when nobody was expecting you and when the lakes and rivers are frozen over. You can often move faster over frozen lakes and rivers and through snow than you can through water and mud.

But, as Napoleon found out when invading Russia during the winter of 1812, an army just cannot do things as well in winter as they can in summer. So invade in spring and summer, and entrench in fall and winter is really the way to successfully invade and conquer Canada in The War of 1812. The weather determines it.

Yet the Americans never managed to figure this out. They were always fighting the calendar. They got going too late. So, as the Russian weather did for the Russians against Napoleon, the Canadian weather did for the British in The War of 1812 against the Americans. And the weather was a handy ally to have.

The sort of swaggering pose in silhouette used by Napolean Bonaparte on battlefields and in famous paintings.

Note: Arms are crossed not stuffed into jacket.

CHAPTER THREE

1812: The First Year Of The War And The One After Which It Is Named

The United States declares war on Great Britain on 18 June 1812. Five days earlier, and without knowing this, Britain repeals the trade embargo on The United States and requests peace talks. This news reaches Greenbush, New York near Albany on 8 August. The American Army there can't do anything about this until the President decides what to do. The President decides on 13 August to reject the request for peace talks and orders the army "to proceed with the utmost vigour . . . gaining possession of the British posts at Niagara and Kingston."

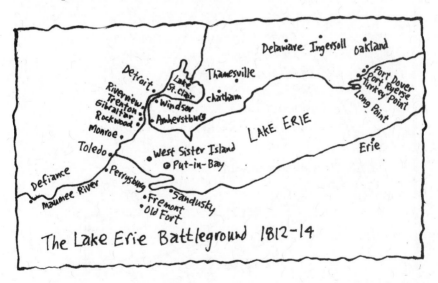

The Lake Erie Battleground 1812-14

The four-pronged attack on Canada seems to have been reduced to a two-pronged attack. The attacks on Amherstburg and Montreal seem to have been forgotten.

Word of the start of the war reaches Montreal on 24 June; Niagara-on-the-Lake on 25 June (where General Brock is); Amherstburg on 28 June; St. Joseph Island on 8 July; and Britain on 30 July. Guards are posted along the north bank of the St. Lawrence River and the west bank of the Niagara River, and the British wait to see where the first American attack will come from. But it doesn't come from Niagara or Kingston as the President ordered. It comes from Michigan.

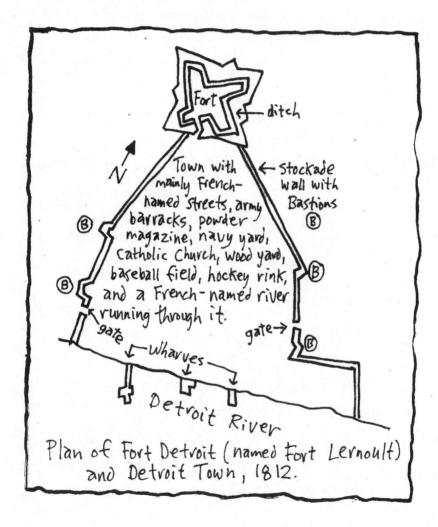

Plan of Fort Detroit (named Fort Lernoult) and Detroit Town, 1812.

The American Invasion of Windsor, Ontario, 12 July – 11 August 1812

Despite being apparently forgotten by their President, the American Army in Dayton, Ohio detailed to invade Canada from Detroit, Michigan and take Amherstburg, Ontario, proceeds north through Urbana, Roundhead, Kenton, Findlay and Perrysburg, Ohio reaching Toledo, Ohio on 30 June. There they put most of their supplies and important military papers on a ship bound for Detroit, and continue on overland north into Michigan.

On 2 July they learn that the war has officially started. On 5 July they reach Detroit and learn that the ship carrying most of their supplies and important military papers has officially been captured by the British from Amherstburg who apparently knew about the start of the war before they did (four days). Now the British have most of their supplies and important military papers, and know all their invasion plans as well.

Detroit, Michigan in 1812 is a four-pointed star fort of earth and wood surrounded by a ditch with 40 cannons and 90 soldiers in it at the corner of Fort Street and Shelby Street in downtown Detroit (fort no longer there); with a mainly French-Canadian village of 160 buildings and 800 people surrounded by a 12-foot-high stockade wall between it and the Detroit River.

When the American Army arrives at Detroit with no food of their own, they quickly eat up all the food Detroit has leaving it with only soap, whisky and ammunition. Detroit is a hungry town; but clean, happy and well-armed.

But needing to find food, the American Army has no choice but to invade Canada to find some, and so the first American invasion of The War of 1812 is launched out of hunger. On 12 June 1812 an American army of 2,000 crosses the Detroit River, lands unopposed on Riverside Drive in Windsor, Ontario (then called Sandwich which makes the Americans feel even hungrier), runs up the flag ("Our flags look extremely well on his majesty's domain"), sets up headquarters in Francois Baby's (Bobby's) house on Pitt Street, issues a proclamation to the Canadian people ("We are an army of friends"), and sets about scouring the countryside for food and burning and wrecking everything else non-edible.

The British in Windsor withdraw south to Amherstburg and Fort Malden (still there). The Americans advance south as far as the Canard River where there is a small skirmish. The Americans go back to Windsor and the British go back to Amherstburg.

Not knowing what to do next the Americans sit in Windsor (they have no experience invading and conquering). They do not feel they are strong enough to attack Amherstburg (defended by 700). They have no cannons. They have no gun carriages for cannons even if they had cannons. There appears to be no corresponding American invasion of Niagara going on at the same time as their invasion, as the Detroit army thought the plan was to be. The American commander dallies. The regular soldiers want to attack Amherstburg but the militia don't. There are Indians all around them (so they think). There are British all around them (so they think). They are surrounded and a long way from home. So they sit. But the British have not been sitting. Brock's offensive-defensive strategy is already underway.

The British capture of Mackinac Island, Michigan, 17 July 1812

St. Joseph Island, Ontario, Canada and Mackinac Island, Michigan, USA, are two islands in the far northwestern end of Lake Huron (the second biggest of the Great Lakes and the fifth largest freshwater lake in the world). Today we would describe them as being in Northern Ontario and Northern Michigan. In

1812 they would be described as being in the back of beyond. Out in the middle of nowhere. Deep in the wilderness. Yet they were the second place The War of 1812 went to.

News of the start of the war reaches the British on St. Joseph's Island on 8 July. The commander has been ordered to attack Mackinac Island if he thinks he can do it. He thinks he can do it. There are 225 British and 410 Indians in Fort St. Joseph. The Indians want to fight. The British want Fort Mackinac. Fort Mackinac is a better fort than Fort St. Joseph (after the British capture Fort Mackinac they abandon Fort St. Joseph and never go back). So on 16 July 1812 the British sail off to capture Mackinac Island from the Americans (50 miles away).

There are 62 Americans in Fort Mackinac on the south shore of Mackinac Island. They don't know the war has started yet. On 17 July the British land on the north end of the island, drag a cannon to the top of an undefended hill overlooking the fort, fire one shot, and ask Fort Mackinac to surrender. It does. The British have captured Mackinac Island. They will hold it until the end of the war. The Indians are happy. They are now committed to fighting for the British. Just what General Brock wanted.

The British Capture of Detroit, Michigan,
16 August 1812

When General Brock in Fort George (Niagara-on-the-Lake, Ontario) learns of the invasion of Windsor and the capture of Mackinac (29 July), he makes sure all is quiet on the Niagara front, and leaves for Amherstburg via Lake Erie, stopping at Port Dover and Long Point and arriving on 13 August.

When the Americans in Windsor learn of the loss of Mackinac Island and the coming of reinforcements for Amherstburg, they get cold feet and that insecure feeling and begin withdrawing back across the Detroit River to Detroit (8-11 August). The first

American invasion of Canada is over. It has lasted only 30 days. And not a lot of conquering has been done.

Brock arrives at Amherstburg two days after the Americans leave Windsor, and meets Tecumseh for the first and only time. Brock says of Tecumseh: "A more sagacious or more gallant warrior does not I believe exist." Tecumseh says of Brock: "This is a man." They agree to attack Detroit together with 730 British, 600 Indians, five cannons and two ships. But the British in Amherstburg have already been busy bothering the Americans in Detroit.

Supplies for Detroit are brought up from Ohio. The British in Amherstburg know this. A supply column is on its way north to Detroit. The British in Amherstburg know this. Detroit sends a relief force of 150 south to meet them. The British in Amherstburg know this and send Tecumseh and 24 Indians across the lake to ambush them. In the vicinity of Parsons Elementary School in Gibraltar, Michigan on Brownstown Creek they skirmish with the

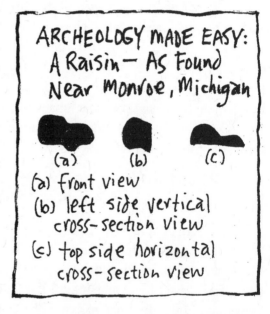

ARCHEOLOGY MADE EASY: A Raisin — As Found Near Monroe, Michigan

(a)   (b)   (c)

(a) front view
(b) left side vertical cross-section view
(c) top side horizontal cross-section view

Americans but are beaten off (5 August). The American relief force marches back to Detroit. The Indians paddle back to Amherstburg. The American supply column stops at Monroe, Michigan on the River Raisin, convinced they can't get through to Detroit because they are surrounded by Indians.

The Americans in Detroit send a second relief force of 600 south to meet the supply column. The British in Amherstburg send Tecumseh and a force of 205 across the lake to ambush them again. In the vicinity of Riverview and Trenton, Michigan they skirmish with the Americans again, but are beaten off once more (9 August). The American relief force marches back to Detroit again after spending "a tentless and foodless night in pouring rain." The British paddle back to Amherstburg again.

The Americans in Detroit send a third relief force of 400 south to meet the supply column. But when they reach the River Raisin the supply column is not there to meet. They've gone back to Ohio. The American relief force marches back to Detroit once again, but doesn't make it this time because while they've been away Detroit has surrendered and been captured, and they've been surrendered and will soon be captured too.

American Army Notebook Showing Indian Count Prior To The Surrender of Detroit, 16 August 1812.

On 15 August General Brock demands the surrender of Detroit otherwise "a body of Indians who have attached themselves to my troops will be beyond control the moment the contest commences." Detroit refuses to surrender and the British begin bombarding the fort.

On 16 August the British assemble at the corner of Sandwich and Chappus Streets in Windsor, cross the river to Gibraltar, Michigan and surround Detroit. The militia put on old British uniforms to look like regular soldiers, and the Indians make lots of noise and run across a field in front of the fort so the Americans can count them. Then they duck into the woods, double back, and run in front of the fort again. Some of them do this three times. Believing they are completely outnumbered and fearing the Indians, Detroit surrenders not only everybody in Detroit, but everybody in Michigan as well, including the third relief force now on its way back north. The British capture 2,182 Americans, 2,500 muskets, 33 cannons (some of which were captured by the Americans from the British at Saratoga, New York in 1777 during The American Revolutionary War), and one ship.

After the capture of Detroit the British also take Fort Wayne (the Fort Wayne in Detroit not the Fort Wayne in Indiana), and Fort Dearborn (the Fort Dearborn in Chicago, Illinois not the Dearborn in Detroit which doesn't have a fort but does have a very nice museum and pioneer village). General Brock hurries back to Niagara expecting the next American invasion to be there. He's right again. But as well as this invasion to come, little bits of war are now breaking out in other places too, and the Americans also make a rather pitiful attempt to recapture Detroit.

An American tavern keeper and two farmers in a rowboat invade Carleton Island in the St. Lawrence River, overcome four British soldiers and two women, and take possession of Fort Haldimand (it's not very big). The island is still American today (New York state), but is privately owned and cannot be visited (it can though still be invaded).

Ninety-five Americans from Cape Vincent, New York raid Gananoque, Ontario on the St. Lawrence River, ransack a house, shoot a woman in the hip, take ammunition and eight prisoners, burn a storehouse, and leave. The British later build a blockhouse at Gananoque.

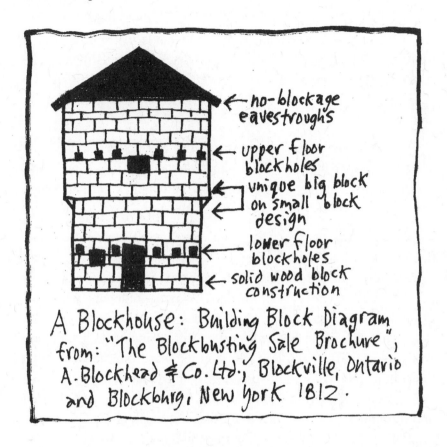

← no-blockage eavestrough's

← upper floor blockholes

← unique big block on small block design

← lower floor blockholes

← solid wood block construction

A Blockhouse: Building Block Diagram from: "The Blockbusting Sale Brochure", A. Blockhead & Co. Ltd.; Blockville, Ontario and Blockburg, New York 1812.

Two hundred Americans from Fort Covington, New York push the British out of St. Regis, New York on the St. Lawrence River, and capture a British flag. The British from Cornwall, Ontario then attack the Americans at Fort Covington, New York.

The British in Prescott, Ontario attack Ogdensburg, New York on the other side of the St. Lawrence River, but are turned back before they reach the shore. The Americans in Ogdensburg really don't want this war, too many Canadians shop in Ogdensburg (during the war two-thirds of the British Army east of Kingston is fed with food bought in New York and Vermont).

Four British ships attack Sackets Harbor, New York but are beaten off. A 32 pound cannonball lands in front of Sacket Mansion and is picked up and fired back at the British. The American Lake Ontario Navy of seven ships chases a British ship back into Kingston harbour, fires on the town, gets fired back at, and leaves.

A British supply convoy on the St. Lawrence River is seized by two American ships near Alexandria Bay, New York. Four British gunboats try to recapture the supplies but are beaten off.

The American general who surrendered Detroit is court-martialled, retired, and replaced by a new general with a new plan to recapture Detroit. It will be a four-pronged attack. Army #1 (2,500), will come east from Fort Wayne, Indiana; Army #2 (1,200), will come north from Urbana, Ohio; Army #3 (3,500), will come down the Sandusky river from Cincinnati, Ohio; and Army #4 (2,000), will follow along in the rear from the west down the Illinois and Wabash Rivers, destroying Indian villages as they go so these Indians can't join the British. It's a very complicated and ambitious plan. And it's starting out at precisely the wrong time of the year for armies to be marching about in this part of the country.

The British however aren't just sitting around in Detroit waiting to be recaptured. They're in Monroe, Michigan and Perrysburg, Ohio heading west up the Maumee River to assist the Indians who have laid siege to Fort Wayne, Indiana. On 25 September the scouts from the British Army of 1,000 going west to Fort Wayne from Detroit, and the scouts from the American Army #1 going east to Detroit from Fort Wayne; meet at Defiance, Ohio. The British retreat back down the river. It rains. Rivers flood. It rains some more. Roads flood. American Army #1 is stuck in Defiance, Ohio. American Army #2 is stuck in Urbana, Ohio. American Army #3 hasn't even gotten to the Sandusky River yet. American Army #4 was on the Wabash River heading east, but then gave up and went home. The American armies are starving, shivering and sick. Soldiers die and desert. Another American general resigns. By 23 October the plan to recapture Detroit is cancelled. They hadn't even reached Michigan yet. They hadn't even conquered Ohio.

The Battle of Queenston Heights, Queenston, Ontario, 13 October 1812

Sir Isaac Brock's Right Uniform Collar (courtesy Fort George Tailors and Dry Cleaners).

General Brock is in Kingston when he learns that the Americans have rejected peace talks. He sails immediately back to Niagara-on-the-Lake (4 September).

The American invasion of Niagara which was supposed to go ahead at the same time as the invasion of Windsor, doesn't get going until well after Detroit has already surrendered and summer is over. And then it uses the army in Albany, New York to attack with, which was supposed to be the army to attack Montreal.

By 29 September the Americans have 6,000 in Buffalo, New York across the Niagara River from Fort Erie, Ontario; and 3,550 soldiers farther north in Lewiston, New York across the Niagara River from Queenston, Ontario. The American commander in Lewiston wants to invade from Lewiston where the river is swift but only 250 yards wide; and the American commander in Buffalo wants to invade from Buffalo where the river is wider but not so swift.

The British have a force of 1,200 spread along the 36 miles of the west side of the Niagara River at Fort Erie and Chippawa (Niagara Falls, Ontario) above Niagara Falls, and Fort George (Niagara-on-the-Lake) below Niagara Falls. They don't know where the Americans will invade from. General Brock thinks they will come across from Fort Niagara (Youngstown, New York) and attack Fort George. They don't. He guesses wrong this time.

The American commanders in Lewiston and Buffalo argue about where to invade from. The commander in Lewiston then decides to invade on his own without the commander from Buffalo. On the night of 10 October 1812, 600 American soldiers march down to the Niagara River at Lewiston (not very quietly either), to launch an invasion of Canada. But some of the boats don't have any oars in them, and it rains very hard, and it's quite dark outside; so the invasion is cancelled.

This invasion attempt though has been observed by the British the whole time, and is thought to be such a pitifully inept surprise invasion attempt that General Brock actually thinks it's probably just a diversionary, distraction invasion attempt only, and that the real invasion will come somewhere else. "An attack is not far distant," he writes in his report on the night of 12 October. He's right. It isn't. In fact it's that very night. And in the very place he didn't think it would be at too.

At 3 a.m. on the morning of 13 October, the first invasion force of 600 American soldiers marches back down to the Niagara River again. This time the 13 boats all have oars in them. The American cannons in Lewiston start bombarding Queenston, and the second major invasion of Canada is underway. Three of the boats drift downriver (it's a very swift river) and two are captured, but the other 10 boats make it across and land above Queenston. This is not a diversionary, distraction invasion after all. This is the real thing.

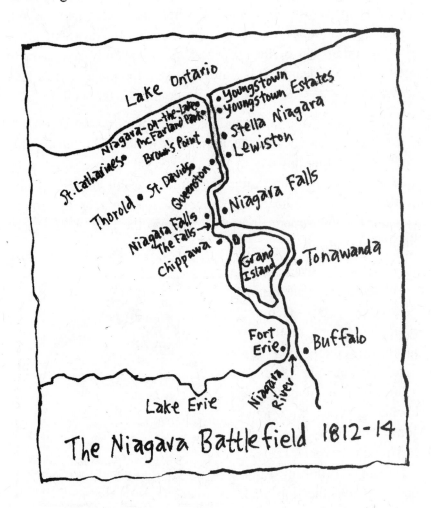

The Niagara Battlefield 1812-14

Queenston in 1812 is a small village of 100 buildings and 300 people (two of which are Mr. and Mrs. James and Laura Secord), with a tall heights to the south of it (or a big hill), defended by 300 soldiers (one of whom is Laura Secord's husband James), and three cannons (one of which is on the heights). When the Americans land above Queenston this means that they land above it on the river, not above it on the map. This is because the Niagara River and Niagara Falls flows and falls up the map, not down it. This always fools a lot of people as it somehow doesn't seem right that water should fall up the map not down it. But there's nothing you or the map makers or anybody else can do about it. The Niagara River flows north up the map. That's just the way things are with the Niagara River and Niagara Falls.

The American commanding officer jumps ashore waving his sword, and is shot in the legs. The British cannon on the heights is shooting down at them. The second American invasion force which is to come after the first invasion force has not invaded yet (the 13 boats are supposed to keep ferrying troops across). But 60 Americans find a path up the heights and start climbing it.

General Brock hears the cannons in Queenston, wakes up Fort George, orders the troops to run to Queenston, jumps on his horse, and rides the six miles to the gun on Queenston Heights arriving at 5 a.m. More Americans are now crossing the river. The 60 Americans climbing the heights reach the top and charge down towards the

General Brock's uniform tunic showing the fatal bullet hole. They got him right between the fourth row of buttons.

British cannon. The cannon is spiked and Brock leads the gun crew down the heights and into Queenston. The British are outnumbered. The Americans hold the heights, but most of their invasion force of 4,200 are still waiting to cross the river. The British troops from Fort George will not arrive in time.

Brock regroups a force of 200 and leads a charge back up the heights. His motto has always been : "Not to ask men to go where I would not lead them." He leads them up the heights and is shot and killed in his red coat with gold epaulettes and decorative Indian scarf given to him by Tecumseh. The British retreat back down the heights, reform, and charge back up the heights again led by the second in command. He is also shot and killed and the British retreat back down the heights again. More Americans are now on top of the heights including Lieutenant-Colonel Winfield Scott who will still be around when the American Civil War starts 49 years later.

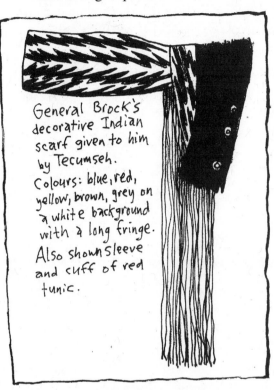

General Brock's decorative Indian scarf given to him by Tecumseh.
Colours: blue, red, yellow, brown, grey on a white background with a long fringe.
Also shown sleeve and cuff of red tunic.

The sort of tightly-restricting neckware worn by Winfield Scott in The War of 1812. It worked. He kept his neck warm and survived the Mexican War and The American Civil War too.

The British reform but do not go charging back up the heights again led by the third in command. Instead they retreat north out of Queenston to await the arrival of the reinforcements from Fort George. The War of 1812 is only 117 days old and already the British have lost their best general and are in danger of losing the first major battle. Things are looking good for the Americans. But are they?

The General Brock Memorial Stone, Queenston Heights. "Near this spot Major General Sir Isaac Brock K.C.B. Provisional Lieutenant Governor of Upper Canada fell on 13 October 1812 while advancing to repel the invading enemy."

The ferry boat system is not working well. Some boats are sunk, some have floated away, some only make one trip. Some American soldiers are in Queenston, some are in Queenston and want to go home, some are still in New York and can't get to Queenston, and some are on top of Queenston Heights and are hungry, thirsty, and running out of ammunition. Some engineers are sent to fortify the heights, but leave their tools behind. Only 1,300 Americans make it across the river. The rest are spectators on the American side.

The British reinforcements from Fort George arrive (550), but instead of charging up the heights they sneak around to the rear where they are met by 300 Indians and the 250 British soldiers from Chippawa. At 3 p.m. the 1,100 British reach the top of the heights and attack the 600 Americans up there by surprise from the rear (from the west). The Americans are trapped. Cliffs and water behind them. Enemy in front of them, including Indians making lots of noise and looking very frightening. At 4:30 p.m. they surrender. The Battle of Queenston Heights is over.

The Americans have lost 300 killed/wounded and 958 taken prisoner. The British have lost 14 killed, but one of them is General Brock, and 77 wounded (one of them is Laura Secord's husband James). The British have won the battle, but lost their general. And The War of 1812 still has two years to go.

The American militia prisoners are sent home (and told not to come back again), the American regular army prisoners are sent to Quebec City (where they can be exchanged for British prisoners), and General Brock is sent to Niagara-on-the-Lake to be buried inside Fort George. Major-General Sir Isaac Brock is actually buried four times. When the first Brock's Monument on Queenston Heights is completed in 1824, he is moved from Fort George and buried there. When this monument is blown up by an Irish dissident in 1840, he is moved to a private burial ground in Queenston and buried there. When the second Brock's Monument is completed in 1856, he is moved again and buried

The rear view of Brock's Monument showing General Brock's 16 foot tall rear view Not showh: circular staircase inside column with 235 stone steps, the 20 foot tall sculpted military trophies at each corner of the base, and the Sub- basement and vaults.

there. And he's still there. Standing on Queenston Heights. Sword in hand. Ready to charge back up the hill.

In Europe in November 1812, Napoleon is retreating from his failed-too-late-in-the-year-invasion of Russia. But in North America the Americans are still trying too-late-in-the-year invasions of Canada.

On 20 November, 400 American soldiers and a new general cross the Niagara River from Buffalo, New York in the morning to invade Fort Erie, Ontario, get cold feet, and retreat back across the river in the afternoon.

At 3 a.m. on 28 November, 1,200 American soldiers from Buffalo climb into boats, are divided into two columns, and cross the Niagara River again towards Canada. Snow is falling and ice is forming on the river. The south column crosses to Fort Erie and lands near Gilmore Road. The north column heads for Fort Erie North near Frenchman's Creek. Some of the south column returns to Buffalo with prisoners, but the rest are captured. The north column is met by cannon fire and returns to Buffalo without ever landing. The Americans put more soldiers into boats and demand that Fort Erie surrenders. Fort Erie declines the invitation to surrender, and the Americans "disembark and dine."

At 8 a.m. on 30 November, 1,500 American soldiers climb into boats to invade Fort Erie again from Buffalo. Then the invasion is rescheduled for 3 a.m. the next day. By dawn on 1 December the boats still have not left yet, and as it is too late in the morning for a surprise night invasion, the invasion of the Niagara Peninsula for 1812 is cancelled altogether. No more tries this year.

The militia go home. The American officers call the American general a coward. The American general challenges an American officer to a pistol duel. They both miss. The American general asks for leave to go home and visit his family, is granted it, and three months later as he has still not returned, is retired from the army and replaced. The Secretary of War is replaced after three others turn down the job.

But just to show that something can be achieved by the Americans in the year of 1812, on 9 December, 100 Americans raid Fort Erie and take two British ships, one of which is successfully brought back to Buffalo.

The Detroit prong of the four-pronged American invasion plan of 1812 has failed. Twice. The Niagara prong has failed. More than twice. The Kingston invasion prong has been forgotten. But there is still the Montreal invasion prong. The Americans have assembled an army of 6,000 at Plattsburgh, New York on the west side of Lake Champlain. On 19 November 1812 they march north to Champlain, New York, near the border, meet a small British force, shoot at them in the dark, and go no further. The New York militia will not leave New York.

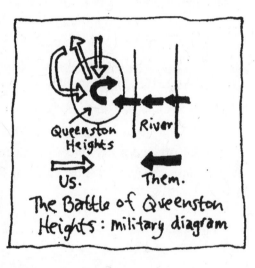

Queenston Heights   River

US.   Them.

The Battle of Queenston Heights: military diagram

On 20 November, 600 Americans leave Champlain, New York to invade Canada and surround the British blockhouse at Lacolle, Quebec. The blockhouse is empty. Not knowing this the Americans fire at each other believing they are firing at the British. Then the British arrive and fire at the Americans, and the Americans retreat back to Plattsburgh. Montreal is safe. The

Montreal invasion prong has failed too. The general in charge asks to be retired from the army and is. Gladly. Good riddance.

At the end of 1812 the British are in Detroit and Fort Mackinac, Michigan, most of the Indians have now decided to join them, and the victory at Queenston Heights has boosted morale and enlistment in the Canadian militias.

"The Glengarry Light Infantry Fencibles will give four guineas bounty and complete set of regimental clothing consisting of: a Regimental Green Jacket, a Cloth Shell Jacket, a Pair of Cloth Pantaloons, a Pair of Shoes, a Regimental Cap, and a Military Great Coat to all who enlist. Note: Socks and Underwear are the responsibility of each volunteer. The Glengarry Light Infantry Fencibles does not get involved with socks and under-wear. We travel Light." (The Kingston Gazette, 11 December 1812).

At the end of 1812 there are no Americans in Canada, except as prisoners of war. It has not been a good year for the Americans. But they will try again in 1813.

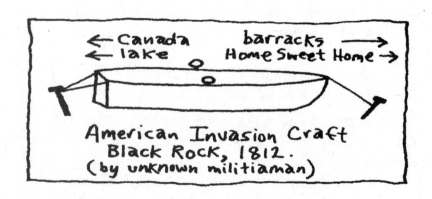

American Invasion Craft
Black Rock, 1812.
(by unknown militiaman)

CHAPTER FOUR

1813: The Second Year of the War

By 1813 the war in Europe is now going badly for the French. Napoleon has lost 480,000 in Russia and is losing in Spain too. But Britain is in no mood to lose Canada. On 9 January 1813 Britain issues a declaration stating that The United States started the war (true), in collusion with France (untrue, but the timing was certainly suspect), in order to take Canada (true).

The British strategy for 1813 is to send reinforcements to Canada whenever they are available, and to blockade and raid the American east coast ports south of New York City, especially Chesapeake Bay (the southern states were more for the war than the northern states were).

The American Army is having the same sorts of problems in The War of 1812 that it had in The American Revolutionary War. Except this time there is no George Washington to make things better. Generals and Secretaries of War keep changing constantly. The militia doesn't cooperate with the regular army. The states are divided over the war. The federal government doesn't financially support the war. The soldiers have poor barracks, poor food, poor uniforms, disease, not enough shoes, and no pay. Congress stalls on all attempts to reform the military. By the end of 1812 the American Army which was supposed to number 30,000 is only 19,000.

The American strategy for 1813 is to enlarge the army for one year only; to take Mobile, Alabama from the Spanish and Canada from the British (two pretty equal tasks); and to divide the army into nine Military Districts under nine generals instead of three Military Districts under three generals. They will capture Kingston and Toronto, Ontario and destroy Fort George and Fort

Erie. In that order. Then the plan is changed. Kingston is too strong to attack, so they will take Toronto and Niagara. But first they will try to recapture Detroit again. And they get an early start on it too.

The Battle of The River Raisin, Monroe, Michigan, 22 January 1813

The four armies of 9,200 that were assembled to recapture Detroit have dwindled to 6,300. On 20 December 1812, 1,000 of the 1,300 Americans left in Army #1 in Defiance, Ohio, proceed east down the Maumee River, reach Monroe, Michigan (a small hamlet of 20 dwellings), and take the small British force of 150 there by surprise (18 January 1813). The British retreat home. But they will soon return.

On 21 January, 1,100 British and six cannons from Amherstburg, Ontario cross the ice on the Detroit River to Gibraltar/Rockwood,

The River Raisin Commemorative Housecoat

- one size fits all ranks
- extra long sleeves to allow for shrinkage
- available from: River Raisin knitting Mills, monroe, Michigan

REMEMBER RIVER RAISIN

Michigan, and the next day take the Americans camped on East Elm Avenue in Monroe, Michigan by surprise. They capture the American general in his housecoat, take 600 prisoners, and the Americans surrender (185 British/367 Americans killed or wounded, only 37 escape). The remaining Americans in Defiance return west up the Maumee River. The British return to Amherstburg. Provoked by an incident, the Indians left behind with the remaining wounded American prisoners kill most of them resulting

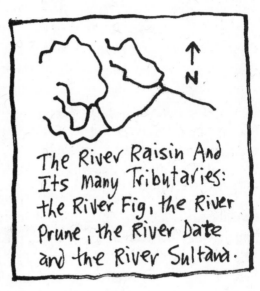

The River Raisin And Its Many Tributaries: the River Fig, the River Prune, the River Date and the River Sultana.

in the famous American political slogan and battle cry "Remember The River Raisin," or "Remember The Raisin." (Over time some people will forget which dried fruit this battle was named after and incorrectly refer to it as "Remember The Date" or "Remember The Fig." But not very often).

In February, despite it still being winter, lots of things are happening in The War of 1812. The Americans return down the Maumee River to Perrysburg, Ohio, build Fort Meigs, collect another army of 4,000, and continue down the Maumee to Toledo to make a daring winter attack on Amherstburg across the frozen ice of Lake Erie. Unfortunately Lake Erie is not frozen over and the ice is breaking up, so the Americans return to Perrysburg for the winter (11 February). There will be no more American attacks on the British in Detroit or Amherstburg just yet. Come spring though, there will be more British attacks on the Americans.

Along the St. Lawrence River the two sides raid each other back and forth across the river. Two hundred Americans from Morristown, New York raid Brockville, Ontario; capture 52 British soldiers, three farmers and a team of horses; set fire to the barracks and leave (6 February). Six hundred British from Prescott, Ontario raid Ogdensburg, New York with small cannons on horse-drawn sleighs; burn the barracks and two ships; and take supplies back across the river. The British promise that there will be no more raids on Ogdensburg if Ogdensburg no longer has any soldiers in it. Ogdensburg does not allow the army back into the town and no longer has any soldiers in it for the rest of the war. Ogdensburg definitely does not have its heart in this war.

As British reinforcements cannot get from Britain to Canada in time to strengthen Kingston, Ontario before an anticipated American attack in the spring of 1813, 550 soldiers of The New Brunswick Regiment are marched overland from Fredericton, New Brunswick to Kingston. They leave on 16 February and arrive on 12 April (700 miles in 56 days using sleighs, toboggans and snowshoes). Their arrival helps persuade the Americans that Kingston is too strong to attack. (Route: St. John River, Madawaska River, Lac Temiscouata, Rivière-du-Loup, St. Lawrence River).

In March 1813 the Russian Emperor Czar Alexander I offers to mediate peace talks between Britain and The United States. The American president eagerly accepts the offer. Britain doesn't. They wait until 14 November 1813 and then send a letter to the American president suggesting direct negotiations without the Russians being involved (Napoleon is defeated at Leipzig in October 1813 and the war is Europe is turning decidedly against the French). The letter doesn't reach the American president until 30 December 1813.

On 17 March the Americans at Buffalo, New York bombard Fort Erie to celebrate St. Patrick's Day.

In April the Americans take Mobile, Alabama from the Spanish. Half the American territorial objectives for 1813 have now been achieved. One down, only Canada to go.

In April as well, both sides begin invading each other again in different places and for different reasons. The British raid Chesapeake Bay, and attack Perrysburg, Ohio because they're running out of food in Amherstburg; and the Americans attack Toronto, Ontario because they don't want to attack Kingston.

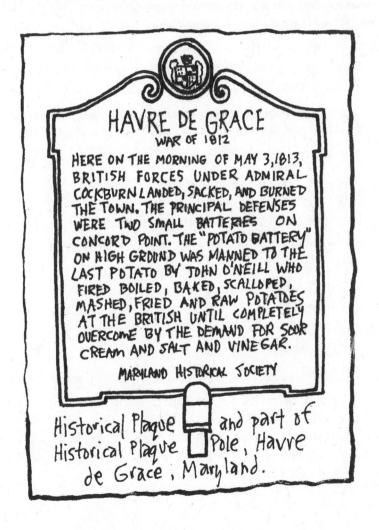

HAVRE DE GRACE
WAR OF 1812

HERE ON THE MORNING OF MAY 3, 1813, BRITISH FORCES UNDER ADMIRAL COCKBURN LANDED, SACKED, AND BURNED THE TOWN. THE PRINCIPAL DEFENSES WERE TWO SMALL BATTERIES ON CONCORD POINT. THE "POTATO BATTERY" ON HIGH GROUND WAS MANNED TO THE LAST POTATO BY JOHN O'NEILL WHO FIRED BOILED, BAKED, SCALLOPED, MASHED, FRIED AND RAW POTATOES AT THE BRITISH UNTIL COMPLETELY OVERCOME BY THE DEMAND FOR SOUR CREAM AND SALT AND VINEGAR.

MARYLAND HISTORICAL SOCIETY

Historical Plaque and part of Historical Plaque Pole, Havre de Grace, Maryland.

From a base on Kent Island, Maryland in the centre of Chesapeake Bay, the British Navy raids the top of Chesapeake Bay (Havre de Grace and Elkton, Maryland); the middle of Chesapeake Bay (Queenstown and St. Michaels, Maryland where only one house is struck by a cannonball that goes through the roof and rolls across the attic floor and down the stairs frightening the occupant Mrs. Merchant); and the bottom of Chesapeake Bay (Norfolk and Hampton, Virginia where the raiding "Canadian Chasseurs" do such a good job looting and burning that the British are embarrassed by their violent and undisciplined behaviour and disband them in 1814). For a change of scenery they also raid Delaware Bay (Lewes, Delaware where a cannonball can still be seen in the basement of a house).

As a result of all these raids in Chesapeake Bay the British learn that Washington, D. C., the capital of The Untied States, is poorly defended. They will use this information later in 1814.

On 25 April the Americans at Sackets Harbor, New York put 1,700 soldiers into ships and sail across Lake Ontario to attack Toronto. They arrive on 26 April, but as they have already been spotted the planned surprise attack on Toronto is postponed until 27 April.

On 26 April the British at Amherstburg put 2,300 soldiers and Indians into boats and canoes and sail or paddle across Lake Erie to attack Perrysburg, Ohio. They arrive on 28 April, and the attack on Fort Meigs begins on 1 May.

Both these attacks have more in common than just the dates. Toronto and Fort Meigs are becoming favourite places to attack. Toronto is easier to attack than Kingston, and Fort Meigs is the closest place to Amherstburg with food. Both sides like attacking these places so much that they will attack them both again in July.

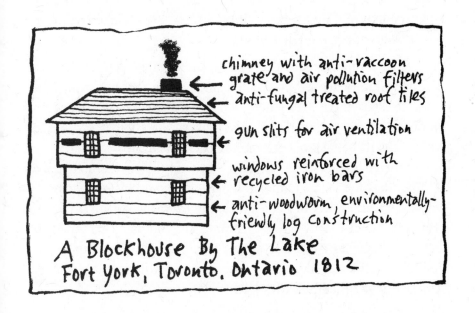

chimney with anti-raccoon grate and air pollution filters

anti-fungal treated roof tiles

gun slits for air ventilation

windows reinforced with recycled iron bars

anti-woodworm, environmentally-friendly log construction

A Blockhouse By The Lake
Fort York, Toronto. Ontario 1812

The First Attack on Toronto, Ontario, 27 April 1813

The first American objective for 1813 is Toronto, the capital of Upper Canada (Ontario). The Americans think Toronto is an important place. It isn't. The British think the Americans might attack Toronto, but as it's not an overly important place it's not overly well defended. Fort York is unfinished. It's a two-storey wood blockhouse, some barracks buildings, a powder magazine (temporary), a Government House with a ditch around it, some cannon batteries along the lakeshore and beside the blockhouse, and 700 soldiers.

To the east of Fort York is York (now Toronto), "a pleasant little town, the houses generally of wood, and containing some good shops, less than one thousand people, and two ships." It also contains the same general features that today's modern downtown Toronto has: harbour and grid-road layout of Front Street (which was then on the harbourfront), Wellington Street, King Street, Adelaide Street, Queen Street, Yonge Street (the longest street in the world), Bay Street, York Street, Simcoe Street, John Street and Peter Street.

The Americans land at 6 a.m. three miles west of the fort on Sunnyside Beach. Some of the small force sent out from Fort York to stop them ("as fine men as the British Army could produce" led by "a remarkably fine-looking man"), gets lost in the woods, the rest attack but are pushed back. The British are heavily outnumbered. They burn the ships, blow up the powder magazine (killing the American commander and more on each side than each side otherwise killed of each other), and retreat east to Kingston (160 miles in 14 rainy days). Toronto surrenders on 28 April (it takes 24 hours to work out the terms of surrender, Toronto has never surrendered before. British 62 killed/92 wounded; Americans 98 killed/222 wounded).

The Americans burn military and government buildings, sack empty houses, annoy the townspeople, take whatever they can carry (including £2,000 and 300 prisoners), destroy what they can't carry, and leave on 8 May (they would have left earlier but they were delayed six days because of bad weather).

This American invasion has lasted only 11 days (six more than they wanted). It was more like a disruptive raid than an invasion. They could have used Toronto as a beachhead to isolate Upper Canada to the west including Burlington, Niagara and Amherstburg; and then advanced east to attack Kingston by land and lake. But they didn't. They get cold feet and leave, dropping off the soldiers at Fort Niagara (Youngstown, New York) "to recruit their health and spirits," and returning the ships to Sackets Harbor. But the Americans will return to Toronto in July. To repeat this rather pointless invasion again.

The First Attack on Fort Meigs, Perrysburg, Ohio, 1-9 May 1813

At the same time as the Americans are invading and not staying very long in Toronto, the British are invading and not staying very long in Perrysburg, Ohio. The Americans are invading because they want to conquer Canada. The British are invading not because they want to conquer Perrysburg, Ohio but because they're running out of food in Amherstburg and it's easier to take food from the other side than it is to wait for food to be delivered to them by their side (little do they know it, but when the Americans attack Toronto they take the food there designated for Amherstburg as well, so Amherstburg has no food to be delivered to them by their side anyway).

Fort Meigs is actually quite a well-constructed fort, situated on the south bank of the Maumee River, just east of The Battle of Fallen Timbers battleground on the opposite bank. It's a fort made up of a 12-foot-high picket fence with a circumference of 2,500 feet set on the top of a dirt wall and enclosing eight blockhouses and four artillery batteries. (The dirt walls come in handy too because British cannonballs get stuck in them and the Americans just gather them up and fire them back at the British. There are a lot of recycled cannonballs in The War of 1812).

From 1-4 May 1813 the 2,300 British outside Fort Meigs bombard the 1,100 Americans inside Fort Meigs with 1,600 cannonballs. But Fort Meigs does not surrender. On 5 May, 1,200 American reinforcements arrive down the river from the west, and there are battles on both banks of the river. The British win the battle on the north bank, and the Americans win the battle on the south bank. Both sides then take 6-7 May off to exchange prisoners, and the British resume bombarding Fort Meigs again on 8 May. But the Indians supporting the British do not like this siege-type of warfare, they prefer fighting warfare, so they leave.

And the Canadian militia wants to get home to their farms, so they want to leave too. And the soldiers are getting sick. And it's raining. So on 9 May the British pack up and go back to Amherstburg empty-handed. And still hungry. The Americans do not follow them. But the British will return to Fort Meigs in July. To try again.

The Battle of Fort George, Niagara-on-the-Lake, Ontario, 25-27 May, 1813

After the invasion of Toronto the Americans drop their no-longer-invading soldiers at Fort Niagara (Youngstown, New York), across the river from Fort George (Niagara-on-the-Lake, Ontario), for R&R ("rest and recover," relaxation didn't enter into it). The ships then go back to Sackets Harbor, New York, pick up more reinforcements, and arrive back at Fort Niagara on 25 May. The attack on Fort George and the Niagara Peninsula of Ontario is underway.

The British have 1,300 inside Fort George. The Americans start bombarding them on 25 May. As Fort George is mainly made of wood a lot of it catches on fire. The British don't know where the Americans will attack from either. They could cross the Niagara River south of the fort, or they could cross the river to the north of the fort and land on the Lake Ontario shoreline west of the fort. They did both. And they attacked Fort Erie at the south end of the Niagara River too. But the main attack is west of Fort George (the fort had been built with all its cannons facing east to defend an attack from the river side of the fort, not the lake/land side to the west).

On 27 May, the Americans land 4,200 at Two Mile Creek on the Lake Ontario shoreline, two miles west of Fort George (Two Mile Creek and all the other Ontario-side Niagara Peninsula creeks flowing into Lake Ontario are named for their distance west from the Niagara River). Two other smaller attacks cross the river from Stella Niagara, New York to Brown's Point, Ontario, north of Queenston and five miles south of Fort George; and from Buffalo, New York to attack Fort Erie at the south end of the river.

The stone powder magazine at Fort George, Niagara-on-the-Lake, Ontario. One of the few powder magazines to shrive the war of 1812, and the only original surviving building at Fort George.

The 170 defenders sent out from Fort George to stop the Americans are outnumbered and they retreat back into the fort. There is a three-hour battle and then the British make a decision. They abandon Fort George, burn most of the buildings that haven't already been burned, blow up the ammunition (the powder magazine is the only stone building in the fort and is not destroyed), and withdraw south to St. Davids (by the inland road not the river road), and Beaver Dams (Thorold, Ontario). At the same time they also abandon Chippawa (south of Niagara Falls, Ontario), and Fort Erie.

The Americans do not go after the retreating British. At least not right away. They enter Fort George at noon, begin rebuilding it, and then go after the British as far as Queenston on 28 May. But the British are not in Queenston, so they go back to Fort George. The Americans who landed at Brown's Point also miss the retreating British. At Beaver Dams the British assemble their troops withdrawn from Fort George, Chippawa and Fort Erie (1,600), and then head west to Burlington Heights, completely abandoning the Niagara Peninsula altogether.

After The Battle of Fort George the American Lake Ontario Navy could have attempted to cut off the retreating British before they could reach Burlington, but the wind did not co-operate. Then comes news that Sackets Harbor is under attack, so the American Lake Ontario Navy takes 2,000 soldiers and sails back to Sackets Harbor. Their cannons have helped to capture Fort George and now the Americans hold the Canadian side of the Niagara River. But the American invasion force is now smaller and has no navy to help protect it.

The Attack on Sackets Harbor, New York, 27-29 May, 1813

On 27 May, while the American Lake Ontario Navy is away helping the Americans capture Fort George, the British Lake Ontario Navy takes 800 soldiers from Kingston, puts them in seven ships and 30 smaller boats, and plans a surprise, sneak attack on Sackets Harbor, New York. But the winds are light and Sackets Harbor spots them before they can land, so it's no longer a surprise, sneak attack, it's just an ordinary attack.

Sackets Harbor is the home port of the American Lake Ontario Navy. It's a well-defended harbour with forts on either side of the harbour entrance. The town itself is protected by log blockhouses, cannon batteries and felled trees, and is defended by 400 regulars and 750 militia. It has a reputation though as an unhealthy place to be, with poor shelter and poor food, and inhabited by "Sackets Harbor Fever" and scurvy, the traditional navy disease, even though the American Lake Ontario Navy spends more time on land than they do on the lake.

With time to organize the town's defence, the American commander guesses correctly where the British will land, so that when they do land on 28 May they are met by three lines of defence between the shore and the town. But the winds are still not cooperating with the British and their ships cannot get close enough to fire on the Sackets Harbor shipyard, their main target. The British infantry though presses forward towards the town, and the

The sort of two-storey, square-on-top-of-triangle fort with big flag that guarded both sides of the harbour at Sackets Harbor, New York 1813.

Americans retreat, set fire to the shipyard, and withdraw back into their blockhouses. After two hours of fighting the British give up trying to take Sackets Harbor and sail back to Kingston on 29 May, just as 450 American reinforcements arrive from Utica, New

York. (The British commander takes a canoe back to Kingston and arrives one day ahead of the ships, the winds not favouring the British in the retreat from Sackets Harbor either).

The Lake Ontario Battleground 1812-14

The most damage done to Sackets Harbor has been of the self-inflicted variety. The Americans put out the fires they set and thus save their own shipyard from themselves.

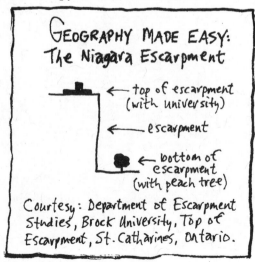

GEOGRAPHY MADE EASY:
The Niagara Escarpment

← top of escarpment (with university)

← escarpment

← bottom of escarpment (with peach tree)

Courtesy: Department of Escarpment Studies, Brock University, Top of Escarpment, St. Catharines, Ontario.

The Battle of Stoney Creek, Ontario, 6-7 June, 1813

After The Battle of Fort George the British retreat west to Burlington Heights (vicinity of Harvey Park, Hamilton, Ontario at the west end of Hamilton Harbour). On 1 June, 2,000 Americans march out of Fort George to go after them. They don't make it. They stop at Forty Mile Creek (Grimsby, Ontario), establish a supply depot, and send for reinforcements. Another 1,000 American soldiers march out of Fort George. By 5 June they are camped in Stoney Creek, Ontario below the Niagara Escarpment. The British are on top of the escarpment watching them.

On the night of 6-7 June, 700 British launch a surprise, sneaky, night bayonet attack on the American camp. But they make too much noise ("the great error was shouting before the line was formed for the attack"), and the attack is not a complete sneaky surprise (but it is at night with bayonets). In a battle of "noise and confusion" in the dark, the British capture two American generals and two cannons, but actually suffer more losses than the Americans (the British commander loses his horse and hat, gets lost, and turns up in the morning horseless and hatless). The British go back to Burlington Heights, and the Americans go back to Grimsby, where they are bombarded by the British Lake Ontario Navy following them along the shore. By 8 June they are back in Fort George again in an "unpleasant dilemma."

The Americans are getting cold feet again. They abandon all the territory they occupy on the Canadian side of Niagara except Fort George. They burn Fort Erie and leave Chippawa and Queenston and all the supplies they had brought over to those places.

The Battle of Beaver Dams, Thorold, Ontario, 24 June, 1813

The Americans have 4,000 (half sick) inside Fort George. They had 6,000 but deserters kept slipping off back home across the river. The British have 3,000 (half sick) in various outposts surrounding Fort George, but they are not strong enough to attack the fort.

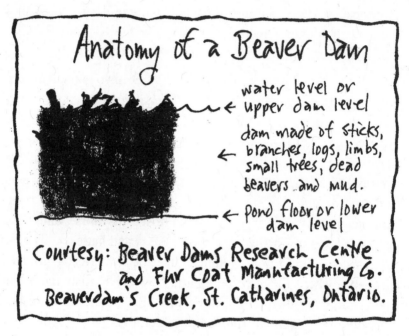

One of these outposts is in the DeCew House at Beaver Dams (vicinity of the Mountain Mills Museum, DeCew Road, St. Catharines, Ontario), commanded by Captain James FitzGibbon. The Americans in Fort George plan a surprise attack on the DeCew House to capture FitzGibbon. They leave Fort George on 23 June with a force of 600 and two cannons and spend that night in Queenston, Ontario. But two days before that some advance

American troops are in Queenston, and it is at this point that Laura Secord enters The War of 1812.

Some American officers enter the home of Laura and James Secord, merchants, of Queenston, Ontario, demanding a meal. Laura overhears them talking. The Americans are on their way from Fort George to capture FitzGibbon at the DeCew House. The British must be warned. She tells James what she has heard. James Secord has a bad knee, the result of being wounded at The Battle of Queenston Heights. "If I crawl on my hands and knees I could not get there in time," he says. "Well, suppose I go?" says Laura. So she does.

At 4:30 a.m. on the hot, humid morning of 22 June 1813, Laura Secord sets off to walk the two and a half miles west to her relative's house in St. Davids. From there she hopes to find somebody else to carry the message on further. But there is nobody in St. Davids to help. So Laura has a rest and at 8 a.m. leaves to make the trip herself. She is wearing a long, brown cotton print dress with little orange flowers on it, a white muslin

Laura Secord's First House Queenston, Ontario. Start of The Laura Secord Walk.

kerchief, a white cotton bonnet, and thin leather slippers. It is the normal walking togs of the day. It is the normal do-everything-in togs of the day for a 38-year-old, five-foot-four-inch mother of five.

Laura Secord's Right Slipper
courtesy: Historical Footwear
Museum, Queenston, Ontario

She walks the 10 miles to Beaver Dams. (Thorold, Ontario. This area is much changed from 1812 due to the building of the Welland Canal and associated lakes and diverted watercourses, but there is still a St. David's Road, Decew Road and Beaverdams Road in Thorold today). It has been raining a lot, the road is muddy, and her slippers keep getting stuck in the mud and coming off.

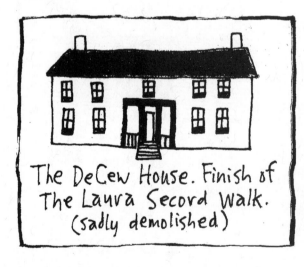

The DeCew House. Finish of The Laura Secord Walk. (sadly demolished)

At Beaver Dams she is not sure of the way further, so she decides to follow the creek west to the DeCew House (part of the Twelve Mile Creek system), rather than take the main road (St. David's Road). For all she knows the Americans may already be on that road. (They aren't. The main body of the American troops has not even left Fort George yet, but Laura Secord does not know this).

After another seven miles of following the creek through woods, fields and swamps, it is early evening when she stumbles into an Indian camp. She has lost her slippers, her dress is muddy and torn, and she is hungry and tired. But the Indians are friendly and they take her immediately to see Captain FitzGibbon.

FitzGibbon believes her story. "This was a person of slight and delicate frame who made this effort in weather excessively warm." He has Laura escorted to a nearby farmhouse where she stays until she returns home the day after The Battle of Beaver Dams (24 June 1813). Then he acts on her information.

The sort of long eyebrows, moustache, beard and sword James FitzGibbon posed with for photographs late in life (1863 or before).

FitzGibbon sends out scouts right away to look for the advancing Americans. If they left Fort George that night or the next day they could attack him tomorrow (23 June). He also alerts his small band of 50 militia and the group of 400 Indians camped near Beaver Dams (the ones Laura ran into) to be ready to move.

It is actually the next night (23 June) that the 600 Americans leave Fort George. They arrive in Queenston at 11 p.m. and set up patrols to stop anyone from leaving the village with information on their whereabouts. But it is too late. Laura Secord left yesterday morning. Captain FitzGibbon already knows they're coming.

At 7 a.m. on the morning of 24 June the Indian scouts from Beaver Dams spot the American troops and inform FitzGibbon. Laura Secord was right. They are on their way. He plans an ambush attack. At a wooded spot along the route in the vicinity of present-day Thorold Stone Road and Davis Road in Thorold, Ontario (not the Beaverdams Battlefield Park site in Thorold), Indians are concealed on both sides of the road.

Then they wait. When the Americans reach the wooded spot, the trap is sprung. The Indians attack from both sides and the rear. FitzGibbon then comes down the road in front with his 50 men and carrying a white handkerchief. The Americans cease fire. FirtzGibbon tells the American commander that they are surrounded. Fearing scalping by the Indians, 462 American soldiers and two canons surrender. Eighty have been killed. The Battle of Beaver Dams is over.

The next day Laura Secord goes home. She is not a hero. Few people know what she has done. She says nothing herself to anybody fearing retaliation from American sympathizers, and she is not mentioned in any official accounts. FitzGibbon is the hero of Beaver Dams. Laura Secord has a crippled husband, a war-ruined business in a war-ruined town, no slippers, and a muddy, torn dress to show for it. Laura Secord is forgotten. (What happens to Laura Secord after The War of 1812 is actually more interesting than her walk. For more on the life of Laura Secord see Appendix: "Laura Secord After The War of 1812").

After the Battle of Beaver Dams the American general in Fort George is replaced "until your health be re-established, and until further ordered." In July the British raid Niagara Falls, New York and Buffalo, New York. By 19 July they have 1,000 troops surrounding Fort George. The Americans in Fort George stay in

Fort George. Nothing much further happens in Niagara until December.

But at the far west end of Lake Erie the British in Amherstburg are getting ready to attack Fort Meigs again. "Our wants are so serious that the enemy must derive great advantage from them alone." In other words, they're still hungry.

The Second Attack on Fort Meigs, Perrysburg, Ohio, 25 July 1813

Tecumseh has a plan to take Fort Meigs. It is not one of his better ideas. A force of 300 British and 3,000 Indians hold a pretend battle near Fort Meigs, trying to trick the Americans inside the fort into thinking that some Americans outside the fort are being attacked, so that those inside the fort will leave the fort to rescue those outside the fort. It doesn't work. The Americans inside the fort know that there are no Americans outside the fort to rescue, so they stay inside the fort, and the British outside the fort use up a lot of ammunition shooting at themselves. With not enough ammunition left to attack Fort

Hats of The War of 1812.

#1. American Light Infantry Regiment. Black stove-pipe with rosette, large two-tone plume and brass plate.

Meigs with for real, the British need something else to attack, so they decide to attack little Fort Stephenson in Fremont, Ohio instead.

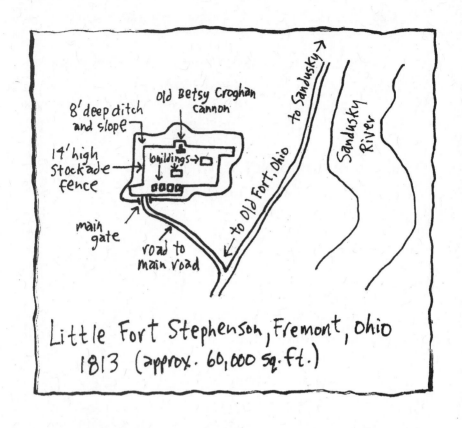

Little Fort Stephenson, Fremont, Ohio
1813 (approx. 60,000 sq. ft.)

The Attack on Fort Stephenson, Fremont, Ohio, 2 August 1813

The British leave Fort Meigs on 28 July, and by 1 August are ready to attack Fort Stephenson. Fort Stephenson is a much smaller fort than Fort Meigs. But the British are a much smaller army now too (down to 600 as 2,700 Indians left after the failure at Fort Meigs).

Fort Stephenson is a few little wooden buildings surrounded by a 14-foot-high stockade fence and an eight-foot-deep ditch, located on the spot of the present-day Birchard Public Library on Croghan Street in Fremont, Ohio. It is defended by only 160

Americans and one cannon nicknamed "Old Betsy Croghan" after the American commander, 21-year-old Major George Croghan. Another 800 Americans are further south up the Sandusky River at Old Fort, Ohio, but they do not come north to reinforce Fort Stephenson because Major Croghan has been ordered to abandon Fort Stephenson. But Major Croghan does not abandon Fort Stephenson and so by disobeying orders he becomes a hero instead of being court-martialled.

The British are desperate to capture Fort Stephenson and its food. They bombard the fort, but their cannonballs only bounce off the walls (the cannonballs were too small rather than Fort Stephenson's walls being too strong). They demand the fort surrender, but it doesn't. So on 2 August they attack it head on. They can't get over the walls or out of the ditch. They lose 96 killed and wounded, do not get the fort, and return to Amherstburg again empty-handed. And still hungry. They didn't get the food they wanted. But then again they now have fewer mouths to feed as well.

An Indian Chief fighting with the British at Fort Stephenson is not impressed with the British soldiers: "They march out, in open daylight, and fight, regardless of the number of warriors they may lose! After the battle is over they retire to feast, and drink wine, as if nothing had happened; after which, they make a statement in writing, of what they have done – each party claiming the victory! They would not do to lead a war party with us. We kill the enemy and save our own men."

A British soldier fighting at Fort Stephenson is not impressed with the American soldiers, other than that they can shoot well: "Their appearance was miserable to the last degree. Cleanliness was a virtue unknown. Their squalid bodies were covered by habiliments that had evidently undergone every change of season, and were arrived at the last stage of repair."

The Second Attack on Toronto, Ontario, 31 July 1813

On 20 July the American Lake Ontario Navy at Sackets Harbor sails down to Fort Niagara, picks up 2,000 soldiers, and heads for the far west end of the lake to attack Burlington Heights. But Burlington Heights looks too strong to attack, so they decide to attack Toronto again instead (31 July). They just attacked Toronto three months ago and it is even more weakly defended now than it was then, but they attack it anyway. In fact most of the soldiers from Toronto are now in Burlington Heights defending it instead of defending Toronto. There isn't much new to sack and burn in Toronto, but the Americans sack and burn what they can find anyway and leave on 1 August, returning to Fort Niagara to drop off the soldiers again. Another pointless invasion. How are you going to conquer Canada if you won't stay there?

It is while they are preparing to return to Sackets Harbor that 13 ships of the American Lake Ontario Navy are confronted by six ships of the British Lake Ontario Navy off Niagara, and what follows is one of the few War of 1812 lake battles. Or in this case, non-battle.

Hats of The War of 1812.

#2.
British 44ᵗʰ Foot.
Beaver or felt Shako with false front, plume feather, brass plate and cord.

Hats of The War of 1812.

#3. American 6ᵗʰ U.S. Infantry Regiment. Black felt stove-pipe with plume.

The War of 1812 Water War

During this war each side has four completely separate navies. An ocean navy; two Great Lakes navies, one on Lake Ontario the lake below Niagara Falls, and one on Lake Erie the lake above Niagara Falls; and one on little Lake Champlain in upper New York State and Vermont.

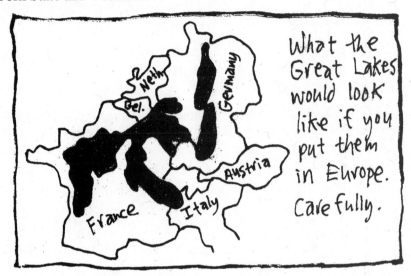

What the Great Lakes would look like if you put them in Europe. Carefully.

Britain's ocean navy controls the ocean over the small American Navy (as much as an ocean can be controlled). They blockade the east coast of The United States from New York City south. There are a number of single-ship ocean naval engagements in which American ships defeat British ships (something unheard of, in a 20-year period of fighting the French Navy the British Navy lost only once), but overall the British control the ocean. In one encounter the British ship *Shannon* captures the American ship *Chesapeake* despite the dying American Captain James Lawrence ordering: "Don't give up the ship!" (which they do anyway, but which goes on to become a famous saying and the motto of the

American Navy), and "Fight her till she sinks!" (which they also don't do, and which goes on to become completely forgotten).

There is a lot of emphasis placed on controlling the Great Lakes during The War of 1812. Too much really. If you control the shore you control the water. Most of the invading is done across rivers anyway, and the St. Lawrence River is the most important waterway to control if you want to control Canada west of Montreal, not the Great Lakes. Troops and supplies are moved around by ships in the Great Lakes, but these lakes are pretty big bodies of water to control with tiny navies.

Lake Ontario is the most important lake. It's the smallest and least great of the Great Lakes, but it's still just slightly smaller than either Wales or the American state of New Jersey, but three and a half times bigger than the Canadian province of Prince Edward Island. On the north side of the lake the British have Kingston, Ontario, the main fortified town west of Montreal and the home port of the British Lake Ontario Navy. On the south side of the lake the Americans have Sackets Harbor, New York, the isolated home port of the American Lake Ontario Navy; and Oswego, New York, the port that supplies Sackets Harbour. Everything for Sackets Harbor has to be sent to Oswego by what is now the route of the Erie Canal. And that was it for Lake Ontario. Three ports and two tiny navies. The two sides together have 11 major vessels on Lake Ontario in 1812, 14 in 1813, and 20 in 1814; with which to control 7,540 square miles of water.

The situation is much the same on Lake Erie. Lake Erie is the 12th largest freshwater lake in the world. A lake just slightly smaller than two Northern Irelands, just slightly larger than the American states of New Hampshire or Vermont, but four and a half times bigger than the Canadian province of Prince Edward Island. On the north side of the lake the British have Fort Erie at the east end of the lake, and Amherstburg at the west end. On the south side of the lake the Americans have Erie, Pennsylvania and Put-in-Bay,

Ohio (Sandusky, Ohio). And that was it for Lake Erie. Four ports and two tiny navies. The two sides together have six major vessels on Lake Erie in 1812, 14 in 1813, and seven in 1814; with which to control 9,940 square miles of water.

But both sides are determined to build more and bigger ships on the lakes than the other side has. The Americans start building a ship at Sackets Harbor, so the British begin building a bigger one at Kingston. The Americans find out about the bigger one at Kingston, so they begin building an even bigger one at Sackets Harbor. The British learn abut the even bigger one at Sackets Harbor, so they begin building an even bigger, bigger one at Kingston. By 1814 the British are transporting ship's frames to Canada to be assembled there, and have plans to build a Lake Ontario ship bigger than any in the Royal Navy; and the Americans have plans to build a Lake Ontario ship bigger than any warship in the world. When the war ends there are four unfinished ships at Kingston and Sackets Harbor.

As it turned out there was one major engagement between the two navies during the war on each lake. One on Lake Ontario and Lake Erie in 1813, and one on Lake Champlain in 1814.

The Non-Battle of Lake Ontario, 7-11 August 1813

On 7 August six ships of the British Lake Ontario Navy catch up with 13 ships of the American Lake Ontario Navy off Niagara. The British ships have mainly short range cannons (called "Carronades" because they were invented by the Carron Iron Company of Scotland), so they want to get within a short range of the American ships and stay away from the American ships' long range cannons. The American ships have mainly long range cannons, so they want to stay at a long range from the British ships and not get within the short range cannons of the British ships.

Although 13 ships against six ships sounds like a mismatch for the Americans, it isn't really. The six British ships are better at

The sort of splashy uniform jacket Isaac "Take No Chances" Chauncey liked to pose for paintings in.

operating as a group, while half the American fleet has to be towed by the other half otherwise they're too slow and can't keep up and the fleet would become too scattered. The American commander is also Commodore Isaac Chauncey, whose main commanding characteristic is that he doesn't take any chances ("Take-No-Chances Chauncey").

The two navies manoeuvre for position. On 8 August two American ships capsize in heavy rain and sink (they are top-heavy with cannons and referred to as "coffins" by their crews). The two navies manoeuvre for position again until the night of 10 August when they harmlessly open fire on each other. Nine American ships break off the engagement and sail away from the British, but two of them turn the wrong way, sail directly into the British, and are captured. On 11 August two more American ships of the remaining nine have to put into Fort Niagara for fear that they will also capsize. The remaining seven American ships then sail back to Sackets Harbor, and the British sail back to Kingston.

After this non-battle the two fleets manoeuvre around for another month skillfully avoiding each other. On 13 September off Rochester, New York, ten Americans ships firing from long range put a hole in one British ship. On 28 September off Toronto, the two sides fire at each other and the Americans lose one foremast and one foretop-gallant mast; and the British lose one main-top mast, one mizzen-top mast, one foretop-mast, and one main-yard, and sail into Burlington Bay to get away from the Americans (this engagement is known as "The Burlington Races"). And that's about it for the water war on Lake Ontario in The War of 1812.

The naval battle on Lake Erie however is a real honest to goodness, blood-on-the-decks, shoot-up-ships, naval battle.

The Battle of Lake Erie
10 September 1813
2 big ships, 3 medium, 1 small and 63 guns
VRS.
2 big ships, 7 medium and 54 guns
(the 9 beat the 6)

The Battle of Lake Erie, 10 September 1813

The Lake Erie navies of both sides are less important than the Lake Ontario navies, and are at the far end of the receiving line for shipbuilding materials, ship builders, and sailors. British sailors for Canada are sent first to Halifax, Nova Scotia, and then from there to Quebec City, from Quebec City to Kingston, and from Kingston to Amherstburg on Lake Erie. Along the way each naval commander at each port keeps what sailors they want and sends the rest on. Amherstburg gets what Kingston sends it, Kingston gets what Quebec City sends it, and Quebec City gets what Halifax sends it. Of 700 sailors sent to Quebec City in 1813, Amherstburg got 45 (and not the cream of the crop either).

The American Lake Erie Navy has the same problem. Promised 740 sailors, the main American Lake Erie Navy port of Erie, Pennsylvania gets 490, including 140 soldiers and other non-sailors. Erie, Pennsylvania in 1813 is "four occupied houses, two of which were taverns"; linked to Pittsburgh, Pennsylvania by 130 miles of "country track;" to Harrisburg, Pennsylvania by 300 miles of "rough road;" and to Philadelphia, Pennsylvania by 425 miles of "turnpike" (which in 1813 meant toll roads).

The British are building one new ship at Amherstburg, and the Americans are building two new ships at Erie. But Erie has a problem. The harbour is protected by a shallow sandbar. Enemy ships can't get into the harbour, but the two new ships can't get out without being lifted over the sandbar without their cannons, and then having their cannons installed on the other side. And the British know this. They blockade Erie so the two ships can't get out. But on 2 August the British ships leave Erie, and after three days of hard work the Americans have the two new ships over the sandbar, their cannons installed, and sailing down to their new Lake Erie naval base at Put-in-Bay, Ohio on South Bass Island near Sandusky, Ohio. From there on 1 September the now complete American Lake Erie Navy sails for Amherstburg to blockade the British Lake Erie Navy for a change.

The British in Amherstburg are in a pickle. They are still short of food and supplies and winter is coming. The British Lake Erie Navy cannot stay blockaded in Amherstburg by the American Lake Erie Navy. They will have to come out, do battle with the Americans, defeat them, and then use the freedom of the lake to attack the American ports for supplies and hopefully bring in some supplies from Long Point, Ontario too. So on 9 September 1813 the British Lake Erie Navy of six ships armed with some cannons from Fort Malden, leaves Amherstburg, and in the vicinity of the Canada/USA border north of West Sister Island in the west end of Lake Erie, the two Lake Erie navies meet for a battle.

1. ~~Oliver Danger Perry~~
2. ~~Oliver Gamble Perry~~
3. ~~Oliver Risk Perry~~
4. ~~Oliver Peril Perry~~
5. ~~Oliver Precarious Perry~~
✓ 6. Oliver Hazard Perry

Mr. and Mrs. Perry Search For A Name For Their New Baby Boy.
from: Mr. and Mrs. Perry's Baby Names List, South Kingston. R.I., 1785.

The American commander Master Commodore Oliver Hazard Perry aboard the *Lawrence* (named for Captain James Lawrence), hoists a flag with the words "Don't Give Up The Ship" on it (the better known of the late Captain Lawrence's last words), and at 11:45 a.m. the nine ships of the American Lake Erie Navy go into battle against the six ships of the British Lake Erie Navy. The situation in terms of cannon strength however, is different than it is on Lake Ontario. The British have more guns, but the Americans have the advantage in both long range and short range cannons. There is hardly any wind that day, but what wind there is favours the Americans and pushes their ships into the British ships.

1. ~~Don't Leave Ship without My Permission.~~
2. ~~Don't Leave The Ship.~~
3. ~~Don't Leave (except on leave).~~
4. ~~Don't Abandon Ship~~
5. ~~Please Don't Abandon Ship~~
6. ~~Don't Give Up The Ship without My Order.~~
7. ~~Don't Give Up The Ship unless you have to.~~
√8. Don't Give Up The Ship.

Oliver Hazard Perry Searches For Words To Put on A New Ship's Flag.
From: The Oliver Hazard Perry Notebook, The Oliver Hazard Perry Museum and Flag Manufacturing Company, Perrysville, Ohio.

The two biggest British ships *Detroit* and *Queen Charlotte* are attacked by *Lawrence*. The British commander is wounded in the leg. *Queen Charlotte's* captain is killed. The British *Little Belt's* captain is killed (another *Little Belt*). The British *Lady Prevost's* captain is wounded in the head. Perry gives up his ship the *Lawrence* (despite his "Don't Give Up The Ship" flag), and transfers in a rowboat to the *Niagara* (taking his "Don't Give Up The Ship" flag with him). The *Queen Charlotte* runs into *Detroit*. The *Niagara* fires into *Detroit*, *Queen Charlotte* and *Hunter* on the one side of her, and *Lady Prevost* on the other side. The British commander is wounded in the arm (he only has one arm to begin with). The first and second in command on each British ship is either killed or wounded. Four British ships surrender. *Chippawa* and *Little Belt* try to escape but are captured. By 3 p.m. it is all over. The American Lake Erie Navy has lost only the *Lawrence*. Four of their ships have seen no action (too slow).

Silhouette of the famous pointing finger from the famous painting of the famous Oliver Hazard Perry famously but hazardously leaving a famous sinking ship for another famous non-sinking ship at the famous Battle of Lake Erie, 10 September 1813.

It is the first time in history that an entire British fleet has been defeated and captured. Perry and his famous flag send out his famous message: "We have met the enemy and they are ours." Perry is a hero. People say that if he had commanded the American Lake Ontario Navy too "there would have been hardly a British ship left on Ontario." The American Navy is so pleased with Perry that they send him to South America where he dies of yellow fever on the Orinoco River of Venezuela in 1819 (they do however put up a monument to him at Put-in-Bay).

Hats of The War of 1812.

#4. British 1st Foot. Black beaver cocked hat with gold lace, black silk bow and regimental button.

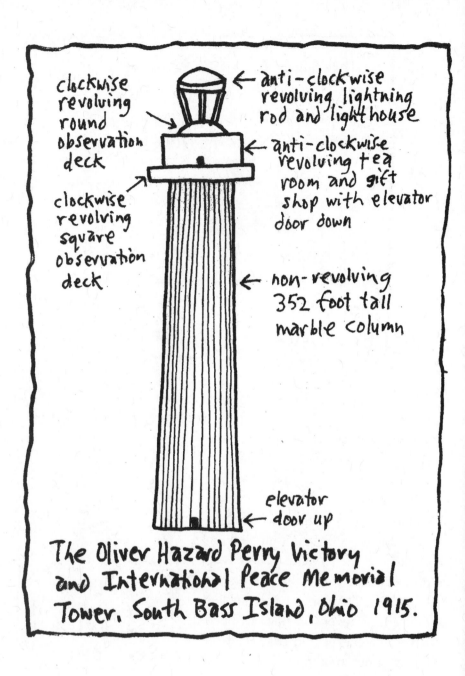

clockwise revolving round observation deck

anti-clockwise revolving lightning rod and lighthouse

anti-clockwise revolving tea room and gift shop with elevator door down

clockwise revolving square observation deck

non-revolving 352 foot tall marble column

elevator door up

The Oliver Hazard Perry Victory and International Peace Memorial Tower. South Bass Island, Ohio 1915.

The Battle of Moraviantown, Ontario,
5 October 1812
(also known as The Battle of The Thames)

The Americans now control Lake Erie. But what will they do with it? They will attack Amherstburg! Finally, they will destroy Fort Malden and little Amherstburg, Ontario that has been the biggest thorn in their side so far in the war. Amherstburg has caused the Americans more problems than any other place in Canada (and a starving Amherstburg at that, just think what Amherstburg could have done if it had been properly fed).

The Americans assemble 5,000 soldiers at Old Fort, Ohio and boats at Put-in-Bay, Ohio; and on 27 September they march and sail to attack Detroit. There are no British left in Detroit. They have abandoned it. The Americans re-occupy Detroit and on 29 September cross the Detroit River below Bois Blanc Island to attack Amherstburg. There are no British left in Amherstburg either. They have abandoned it as well. In fact the British have abandoned the whole of the west end of Upper

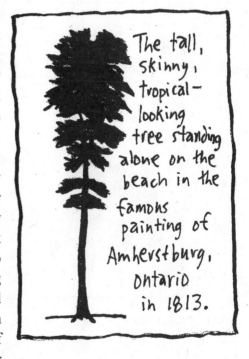

The tall, skinny, tropical-looking tree standing alone on the beach in the famous painting of Amherstburg, Ontario in 1813.

Canada. The Americans occupy Amherstburg and will stay there for the rest of the war. It will be their prize. Their only prize.

The British have left Detroit and Amherstburg just in time. They abandoned Amherstburg on 23 September and Detroit on 24 September, and 900 soldiers and 1,200 Indians under Tecumseh begin retreating east along the south shore of Lake St. Clair to Lighthouse Cove, Ontario at the mouth of the Thames River. From here they will go east up the Thames River valley to Burlington Heights. The Indians don't want to retreat, they want to fight. The British want to retreat, but they need the Indians, so they promise that somewhere along the way they will stop and fight the Americans. They keep their promise.

The Americans decide to go after the British on 10 October with an army of 3,500 including 1,500 "Kentucky Cavalry" in top hats and black shirts with red fringe, who are very good at yelling the battle cry "Remember the River Raisin!"

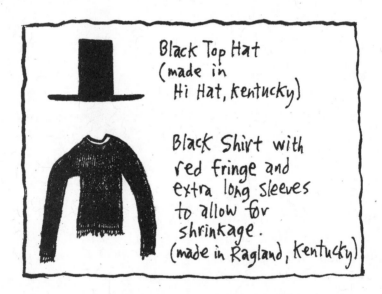

Black Top Hat (made in Hi Hat, Kentucky)

Black Shirt with red fringe and extra long sleeves to allow for shrinkage. (made in Ragland, Kentucky)

The British retreat is slow. The Americans catch up to them at Chatham, Ontario on 4 October and there is a small skirmish there in which the British lose their ammunition wagons. The British keep retreating east. But they promised the Indians that they will stand and fight the Americans and very soon they do. On 5 October near the Moraviantown Indian village east of Thamesville, Ontario, at a spot on the road with the river on one side and woods and swamp on the other side, the British stop. They line up across the road with their one cannon in the middle of the road and Tecumseh and the Indians in the woods and the swamp, and wait for the Americans. They only have two hours to wait.

HERE ON OCTOBER 6, 1813 WAS FOUGHT THE BATTLE OF THE THAMES AND HERE TECUMSEH FELL

ERECTED BY THE CITIZENS OF THAMESVILLE A.D. 1911.

Inscription on the Tecumseh Memorial marker near Thamesville, Ontario.

The Kentucky Cavalry in top hats and black shirts with red fringe, charge the British on the road and the Indians in the woods and swamp yelling "Remember the River Raisin!" It works (one young officer yells "Remember the River Prune!" but is quickly corrected by his colleagues and never makes the same mistake again). The British fall back, their one cannon not having been fired; and the Indians fall back, Tecumseh having been killed. It's all over in ten minutes. Only 276 British soldiers and 400 Indians escape. Also present at The Battle of Moraviantown is Ohio Militia officer Charles Sherman, who later names his third son after Tecumseh. William Tecumseh Sherman will make a name for himself in The American Civil War. Both Canada and The United States will also name a town after Tecumseh (Tecumseh, Michigan; Tecumseh, Ontario).

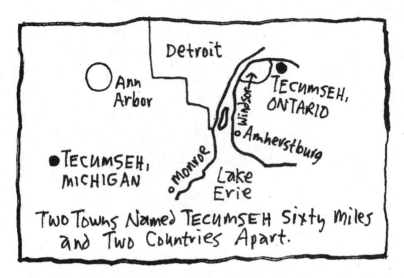

Two Towns Named TECUMSEH Sixty miles and Two Countries Apart.

The Americans do not go after the retreating British. They are still 150 miles west of Burlington Heights and it is too late in the season to invade any farther inland, so they go back to Detroit.

The triumphant American general receives a hero's welcome in Buffalo, Sackets Harbor, New York City, Philadelphia and Washington. The American Army is so pleased with him that he is reassigned to Cincinnati, Ohio. He resigns, has his resignation accepted, and leaves the army. The British general is recalled to Britain, court-martialled, and retired. You win, you lose; you lose, you lose. The War of 1812 is not kind to generals. You're either cashiered, court-martialled, castaway or dead.

The Americans now control Ohio, Michigan and the west end of southern Ontario, and have signed peace treaties with the Indians effectively taking them out of the war. Things are looking up again for the Americans. But are they? What are they going to do with it? It might have been late in the season to attack Burlington

Heights from the direction of Moraviantown, but it could still be done from Niagara. After Detroit, Windsor and Amherstburg are garrisoned, the rest of the Detroit army (1,200) are taken to Buffalo and the Fort Niagara. They want to attack Burlington Heights, but they are taken to Sackets Harbor instead.

The Lake Champlain Battleground 1813-14

The favoured target for the Americans for the end of 1813 is not Burlington Heights but Montreal. It used to be Montreal and Kingston, or Montreal or Kingston, but as the American Lake Ontario Navy under Chauncey does not want to take a chance attacking Kingston, it will now be just Montreal. It will be a two-pronged attack. A west prong going east down the St. Lawrence River from Sackets Harbor, New York; and an east prong going north down the Richelieu River from Plattsburgh, New York.

The west prong of 7,000 soldiers, 60 cannons and 350 boats will assemble on Grenadier Island, New York near the St. Lawrence River, and leave there on 15 September. But on 15 September the Detroit army has not even invaded Canada yet to have their men available to be transferred to Sackets Harbor. And it's now getting late in the year to be invading. And on top of that, the generals of the two prongs and the Secretary of War do not get along and do not agree on strategy. The east prong general will not take orders from the west prong general, only from the Secretary of War, and he notifies the army that he will resign from the army after this campaign is over anyway. The west prong general wants to attack Montreal, but the Secretary of War wants to attack Kingston. Then the west prong general wants to attack Kingston, and the Secretary of War wants to attack Montreal. The result is that by mid-October nothing is attacked and the west prong does not actually leave Sackets Harbor for Grenadier Island until 17 October. Through snow and storms. Thirty boats sink. This is not the kind of weather to be invading Canada in.

The British start preparing for an attack along the St. Lawrence River in September. They reinforce Kingston and Montreal, and set up posts along the St. Lawrence at Gananoque, Prescott and Cornwall, Ontario; and in Quebec at Lachine and Saint-Pierre north of the river, and Chateauguay, LaPrairie, Saint-Phillippe, L'Acadie, Saint-Jean-sur-Richelieu, I'lle-aux-Noix and

Hemmingford south of the river. Church bells are organized to ring warnings, spies are organized to spy, sniping parties are organized to snipe, and the militias are drilled and armed with guns from Britain and blue toques and voyageur songs from Quebec. The American invasion of late 1813 will not be a surprise invasion.

The east and west prongs both end up in battles before even getting close to Montreal. And both never reach Montreal. The east prong's battle comes first.

The Battle of Chateauguay, Ormstown, Quebec, 26 October 1813

The east prong of 5,500 soldiers and ten cannons marches north from Plattsburgh on 19 September, right on schedule with the original timing of the west prong to be entering the St. Lawrence River on 15 September. But the west prong is seven weeks behind schedule. Now the east prong falls behind schedule too.

They cross the border from Champlain, New York at night and near Lacolle, Quebec meet a small force of Canadian militia and Indians. They shoot at them, get lost in the woods, shoot at each other in the dark, and retreat back across the border. The next day they march north again and meet a force of 900 British which they think is considerably larger that that. The soldiers complain about the dangers of dying by Indians, and the general complains about the dangers of dying by thirst (all the wells and streams are dry), and so the east prong goes back to Plattsburgh.

The east prong now changes its direction of attack. Instead of going north down the Richelieu River they will go west to the Chateauguay River, then north down it to Montreal. It's 70 miles farther, but hopefully there will be no Indians and lots of water along the way. They leave on 23 September. At Chateauguay, New York they are ordered to halt because the west prong has not even started yet. (There are lots of Chateauguays in The Battle of Chateauguay. There are the town of Chateauguay, Quebec and Chateauguay, New

York, with the Chateauguay River and The Battle of Chateauguay between them).

While waiting at Chateauguay, New York the east prong repairs the road to Plattsburgh (the east prong general is actually more keen on being a road engineer than a general), eats up their supplies, sends to Plattsburgh for more supplies, and drills. A small raid is sent from Burlington, Vermont to Philipsburg, Quebec on Lake Champlain, which captures supplies and the townsfolk "surprised in their beds" (11 October).

On 19 October the east prong is ordered to begin advancing north again. At this point the west prong is just leaving Sackets Harbor for Grenadier Island. There is snow on the ground. On 21 October, 4,000 American soldiers cross the border along the Chateauguay River (1,500 New York Militia refuse to cross the border and don't). Ironically the east prong is now just 17 miles east of where the west prong will eventually end up (Fort Covington, New York). On 23 October they stop at Ormstown, Quebec. On 25 October they move along the north bank of the river and 3½ miles east of Ormstown they meet the first line of defence of 1,500 British and Canadian Militia waiting for them under the command of Lieutenant Colonel Charles-Michel d'Irumberry de Salaberry, a 35-year-old veteran of the British Army with a very long French-sounding name who has recently been fighting Napoleon in Europe.

Along the north bank of the Chateauguay River the British have constructed a series of five defensive barricades behind five streams running into the river, with the last of these at the only place the river can be crossed; along with one defensive line on the south bank of the river near this crossing.

The Americans send 1,500 troops to the south side of the river to secretly outflank the British and attack them on the morning of 26 October. The south bank is swampy and heavily treed. The river here is 40 yards wide and five-six feet deep. The outflanking force has to go 15 miles out of its way to cross it. They get lost in the dark. It rains. The British send a force to the south bank to meet them. When daylight comes on 26 October the American secret outflanking force is directly opposite the British on the other side of the river, in full view, and no longer a secret (they never were).

The Americans on the north bank have been waiting for the secret outflanking force on the south bank to secretly outflank. But they haven't outflanked and they're not a secret, and they're being attacked from both straight ahead and across the river. They retreat. The British shout, cheer, blow bugles and otherwise make lots of noise to give the impression that there are more of them than there are (the same trick used by Tecumseh at Detroit). It works. The American north bank force charges, sees the south bank force retreating, and retreats too. All the way back to Chateauguay, New York. "I have won a victory mounted on a wooden horse," says de Salaberry, who later has Salaberry-de-Valleyfield, Quebec named after him.

Only 50 Americans and five British have been killed. The American north bank force hardly did anything. For the second time the east prong has been turned back by a heavily outnumbered force. Two days after the Battle of Chateauguay the west prong leaves Grenadier Island. At Chateauguay, New York the east prong is ordered to meet the west prong at St. Regis, New York (only 30 miles west of where they are now), and to bring along enough supplies with them for both armies (8 November). But the east prong hardly has enough supplies for themselves let alone two armies, so they go back to Plattsburgh instead and the east prong general resigns, as he said he would do in the first place. He is recalled to Washington under arrest and allowed to retire, which is what he wanted to do all along. The east prong of The Montreal Invasion of 1813 is defeated. But this leaves the west prong rather out on its own.

The Battle of Crysler's Farm, Morrisburg, Ontario, 11 November 1813

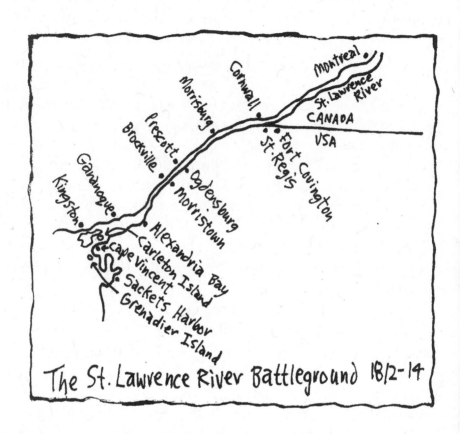

The St. Lawrence River Battleground 1812-14

The west prong leaves Grenadier Island on 28 October. The 320 boats in a flotilla five miles long float down the south channel of the St. Lawrence River. Fifteen miles across on the other side of Wolfe Island the British in Kingston put 800 soldiers and three cannons into nine boats and follow them. On 1-2 November they fire on the Americans camped at Clayton, New York.

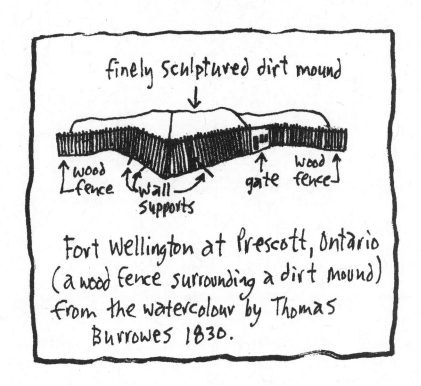

finely sculptured dirt mound

wood fence · wall supports · gate · wood fence

Fort Wellington at Prescott, Ontario (a wood fence surrounding a dirt mound) from the watercolour by Thomas Burrowes 1830.

On 6 November the American Army is unloaded west of Ogdensburg, New York, the empty boats drift past Prescott, Ontario and are shot at by Fort Wellington, and the army is loaded up back into the boats again east of Ogdensburg. On 9 November they land 1,500 soldiers on the Canadian side to secure the river for the passage of the boats through the Long Sault Rapids. (The St. Lawrence River has changed a lot since 1813 due to the completion of the St. Lawrence Seaway in 1959. Rapids, seven "Lost Villages," and most of the Crysler's Farm battlefield are now under 28 feet of water. Crysler Hall, the home of the Crysler family on whose farm the battle was fought, was preserved and is now in Upper Canada Village near Morrisburg Ontario, along with a Crysler's Farm Battlefield Park).

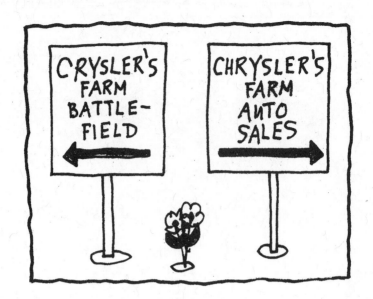

On 10 November the Americans set up headquarters on the Canadian side at Michael Cook's Tavern. To the west of them the British (now 1,200) set up headquarters at John Crysler's farm (the Americans have the more fun headquarters). The next day is dull and cold with rain and sleet (but what do you expect in Canada on 11 November?). The British look out east over an open field (partly ploughed, partly winter wheat), two gullies and a deep ravine. To their right is the river. To their left dense woods and swamp. They are behind a cedar log fence. Some of them are in the gullies. Straight ahead on the other side of the field, gullies and ravine are the Americans. Their commander and their second in command are both too sick to command. The commander is on his boat. Many of the soldiers are tired, sick, cold, hungry and don't feel very well either; but they don't have a boat to go and lie down in.

At 8 a.m. the Americans charge across the muddy field, but are stopped by the British behind the cedar log fence and their cannons and gunboats. The Americans advance along the edge of the dense woods and charge, but are stopped by the British who quickly reform to face north instead of east and so are not encircled.

The American cavalry charges down the river road, but are stopped (one cavalry officer jumps over the cedar log fence but finds himself all alone on the other side and jumps back over the fence again). Three times the Americans charge, and three times they are stopped. "The Americans come on in a very gallant style." The American officers second and third in command are killed. The British charge the Americans and the

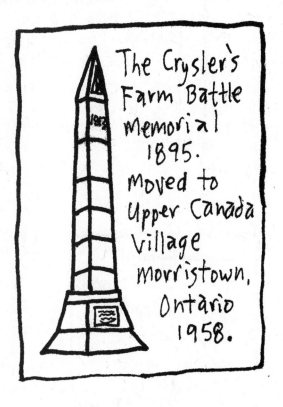

The Crysler's Farm Battle Memorial 1895. Moved to Upper Canada Village Morristown, Ontario 1958.

Americans retreat. At 4 p.m. the British capture the American cannons and the Americans begin retreating back across the river to the American side.

The west prong of The Montreal Invasion of 1813 goes through the rapids and east down the St. Lawrence River to St. Regis, New York where they are supposed to meet the east prong with enough supplies for all of them. But the east prong is not there and has already gone back to Plattsburgh. The west prong has been defeated too. The Montreal Invasion of 1813 is cancelled altogether.

The west prong spends a terrible winter in Fort Covington, New York, where more soldiers die of disease than died on the

Crysler's Farm battlefield (pneumonia, diarrhea, dysentery, typhoid, rotting limbs). The American commander convalesces in Malone, New York, and is later court-martialled, acquitted, and retired. In the spring what is left of the west prong army is split up, half going to Plattsburgh and half going back to Sackets Harbor.

The Battle of Crysler's Farm is a different kind of battle than the other battles of The War of 1812, because it was fought solely in an open field, European-style, where the parade ground manoeuvres of the British "thin red line" could really shine. And shine they do. American losses: 102 killed, 237 wounded, 100 prisoners/British losses: 22 killed, 148 wounded, 9 missing (their descendants probably living somewhere today in Stormont, Dundas and Glengarry County, Ontario). The secret to the "thin red line" was its training and the fact that it was actually two lines. Two lines of soldiers one behind the other waiting until the enemy was within 100 yards range of them before firing. Waiting while being shot at by the enemy. Each soldier could fire three rounds per minute, or one every 20 seconds. The two lines together alternating fire could deliver six rounds per minute, or one every 10 seconds. Devastating. How far can you run in 10 seconds? An enemy advancing against them, or being advanced upon, would be intimidated by their reputation, their red uniforms, their order, and their calmness. When the British finally started firing they just mowed down everything standing in front of them. The only way you could get past them was by overwhelming numbers. Then once the British got the enemy retreating, they charged after them with bayonets. This is what beat Napoleon and make the British army the best in the world at this time.

A "Thin Red Line" (as seen depicted by a rather thickish black one).

But, put this type of fighting in North America and things did not always turn out as well as they did at Crysler's Farm. During The American Revolutionary War the British did not adapt very well to the changed conditions (The Battle of Bunker Hill). They could win battles, but they couldn't win the war. They tried to conquer territory instead of trying to conquer the American Army, and they didn't do a very good job of it. The Americans on the other hand didn't care about territory and just tried to keep their armies alive, and did a good job of it.

In The War of 1812 however the conditions were very much the same, but the situations of the two sides were reversed, and the British did much better. The Americans were trying to conquer territory, but didn't do a very good job of it; and the British were trying to stop armies, and did a good job of it.

The Capture of Fort Niagara, Youngstown, New York , 18-19 December 1813

In November 1813, the 1,600 Americans in Fort George (Niagara-on-the-Lake, Ontario), decide to attack Burlington Heights again. They get as far as St. Catharines this time, when they learn of the defeat of the Montreal Invasion to the east (28 November). They also learn that 600 of their own army have already gone back to New York without permission. The rest of them figure that this isn't such a bad thing for them to do either, so they return to Fort George and on 10 December burn the fort and 130 of the 300 buildings in Niagara-on-the-Lake, and cross

Part of The French Castle, Fort Niagara, Youngstown, New York as it looked in 1812 (the roof was removed and two cannons placed on top).

the river to Fort Niagara. Home sweet home. But not for long.

Fort Niagara is a much older and better built fort than its neighbour Fort George. It's 114 years older and more of it is made of stone (the fort's best feature is the stone "French Castle"). Originally built by the French in 1682, it was taken over by the British in 1759, and claimed by the Americans in 1796. It's a difficult fort to attack, defended by 29 cannons, three towers, bastions, palisades and ramparts. But in late December 1813 it's defended by only 450 American soldiers, 50 of whom are sick (the rest of the New York Militia from Fort George went home on their 9 December discharge date). And, as things turned out, the fort was actually captured quite easily by the British.

The British plan a surprise, sneak, night attack on Fort Niagara. They bring boats overland from Burlington Heights (42 miles), and on the night of 18-19 December, 562 British assemble at the McFarland House on the Niagara River south of Niagara-on-the-Lake (McFarland Park), and cross over to Youngstown Estates, New York, 2½ miles south of Fort Niagara. There's snow on the ground. At 3 a.m. they use the fort's password they've learned, and bayonet charge through the main gate killing 65 and capturing everything else inside (7,000 muskets, 7,000 pairs of shoes, 350 prisoners, the 29 cannons, and a whole lot of clothing much of it originally captured by the Americans from the British).

At 5 a.m. a cannon shot from the newly-captured Fort Niagara signals 1,000 British and 500 Indians to attack Lewiston, New York, which they do. They also destroy Youngstown, Niagara Falls and Tonawanda, New York and everything in between, including four ships. On 30 December having interrupted their invasion to cross back over to the Canadian side for Christmas, they return to where they left off and loot and burn 333 buildings in Buffalo, New York (the Black Rock Canal/Ferry Street area). By the end of 1813 both sides of the Niagara River are not a pretty sight. By the end of 1813 the American accomplishments for the war are not a pretty sight either. They have conquered Amherstburg,

Ontario. And that's it. Not much to show for two years of invading. And over on the west side of the continent they've lost too. It's just happened a whole lot slower over there. And a whole lot quieter.

Astoria, Oregon, 13 December 1813

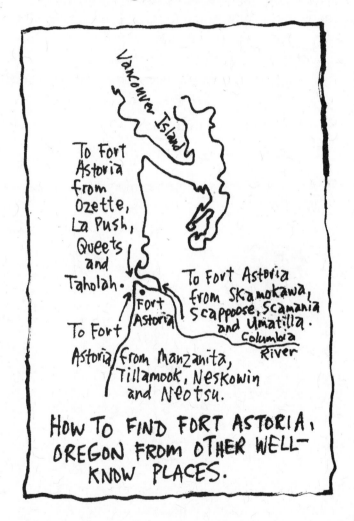

The Americans in Fort Astoria on the Columbia River in Oregon Territory not far from the Pacific Ocean, don't learn about The War of 1812 until 15 January 1813. Threatened with the arrival of the British Navy to take over the fort, the American Pacific Fur Company sells Fort Astoria to the Canadian North West Company (16 October 1813), and then carries on business as normal. When the British ship *Racoon* arrives on 13 December 1813, the Union Jack is already flying over Astoria, and all they have to do is claim the country in the name of the King, and change the name of the fort to Fort George in honour of the King (the other Fort George in Niagara-on-the-Lake is over 2,000 miles away so the thought that the two Fort Georges might get mixed up never crosses their mind).

On 30 December 1813 the letter sent by the British to the American President on 4 November 1813 suggesting direct meetings to negotiate a peace settlement, finally arrives. The Americans reply on 5 January 1814 suggesting meeting in Gothenburg, Sweden; and then they choose four negotiators and send them to Gothenburg, Sweden where they arrive on 13 April 1814. But the British do not want to meet in Gothenburg, Sweden. The Americans then propose meeting in Amsterdam, Holland, and the British propose meeting in Ghent, Belgium. The Americans accept Ghent, Belgium and move their four negotiators from Gothenburg, Sweden to Ghent, Belgium where they arrive on 24 June 1814. The British negotiators don't arrive in Ghent, Belgium until 6 August 1814. And the unofficial peace treaty, which becomes the official peace treaty, doesn't arrive until another four-and-a-half months after that.

Hats of The War of 1812.

#5. British 42nd Foot.
Hummel bonnet with black ostrich feathers, cockade, regimental button and red and white plume.

CHAPTER FIVE

1814: The Third and Last Year of the War

In 1813 in the war in Europe, Napoleon having lost 480,000 of an army of 600,000 in Russia, loses another 68,000 at The Battle of Leipzig (16-19 October 1813), and is only six months away from being defeated for the first time and sent to exile on the island of Elba (11 April 1814).

The British strategy for the war in North America is to force the Americans "to sue for peace." Thirteen thousand more troops are sent to Canada from Spain. Two-hundred-and-fifty sailors for Kingston, Ontario are marched overland from New Brunswick during the winter just like the soldiers were the year before (they take 53 days to make the trip, three days less than last year because of "the unusually mild weather during the entire of this winter"). Six hundred more sailors and four prefabricated ships are sent to Quebec City. Three of the ships stay in their crates, one is delivered to Kingston in July 1814, but isn't assembled until December when the war is almost over. The military targets for 1814 will be Sackets Harbor and Plattsburgh, the holding of the American side of Niagara, and the recapture of Detroit. The British Navy will also send "a considerable force" against the American east coast. Sailors are recruited with the promise that "you will be comfortably and genteely clothed," and that "Every Thing That Swims The Seas Must Be A Prize!"

The British will have 16,000 troops in North America in 1814. The Americans are supposed to have an army of 58,000, but they actually have only 24,000, and they really only have 12,000 because half of the 24,000 have their terms of service expire. This is not a big American army, and it never is.

The American strategy for the war is equally confused. They don't know which part of Canada to attack. They want to recapture Fort Niagara and Mackinac Island, and to attack Burlington Heights and Toronto (for some unknown reason), while at the same time marching north from Plattsburgh to Montreal again (to give it that good old college try). And they really want to attack Kingston, but they don't think they're strong enough to attack Kingston (they never are and they never do). The Sackets Harbor Army won't sail with the Sackets Harbor Navy until the Sackets Harbor Navy has control of Lake Ontario, which they don't have and which they never do either because they won't attack Kingston. The American Lake Ontario Navy is too busy building ships to keep up with the shipbuilding in Kingston, instead of sailing the ships they've already got and trying to sink the ships in Kingston. The naval war on Lake Ontario is a shipbuilding war, not a ships-on-the-lake-shooting-at-each-other war.

So, by the process of elimination, the Americans will attack Niagara again (the Niagara region gets picked on the most in this war). However they don't get around to formulating this plan until 30 April 1814, and they don't get Presidential agreement for this plan until 7 June. Half the year is already over by then. As a result most of the action in The War of 1812 in the first half of 1814 is of the relatively small, local initiative variety.

British from Cornwall, Ontario raid Fort Covington, Malone, Chateauguay, Hopkinton and Madrid, New York (6-24 February 1814).

Americans (165) from Detroit raid east up the Thames River valley past the site of The Battle of Moraviantown, but are met by 240 British from Delaware, Ontario at The Battle of The Longwoods west of Delaware. The British attack the Americans but are beaten back and return to Delaware. The Americans return to Detroit (4 March 1814). Americans from Amherstburg, Ontario raid Ingersoll, Ontario and return to Amherstburg (August 1814). Americans from Detroit raid east again heading for Burlington Heights once more. They skirmish with Canadian militia at Oakland, Ontario, south of Brantford, can't get across the Grand River, and return to Detroit (26 October 1814).

One reason the Americans are raiding southwestern Ontario is the same reason the British attacked northern Ohio: food. Both Detroit and Amherstburg are lightly-settled, subsistence agricultural areas that have had occupying armies in them since the war began, and they don't have any food left. So if you haven't got any food where you are, you go and find food somewhere else. So if you're Americans, you raid Canada.

Four thousand Americans and 11 cannons march north in deep snow from Plattsburg, New York and attack the mill and blockhouse in Lacolle, Quebec defended by 180 British. But as it's getting dark, and as the weather looks threatening, and as British reinforcements might arrive anytime soon (they don't), and as the British don't seem to be running out of ammunition (they are), and as their cannons are having no effect on the thick stone walls of the mill; the Americans go back to Plattsburgh (30 March 1814).

Two things happen though as a result of this otherwise unremarkable little battle in Quebec. The first thing that happens is that the American general in charge is relieved of his command as part of the American Secretary of War's clearout of American generals. Five old generals out, nine new generals in. The President is now responsible for approving war strategy (this reorganized military structure lasts until the start of The American Civil War 1861-1865).

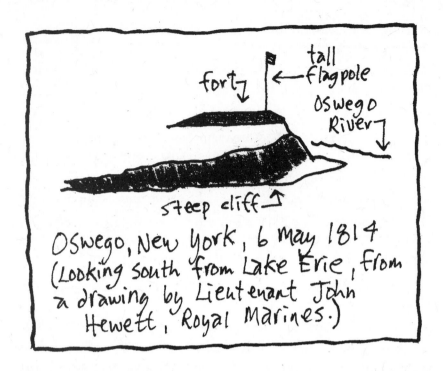

forty

tall flagpole

Oswego River

steep cliff

Oswego, New York, 6 May 1814 (Looking south from Lake Erie, from a drawing by Lieutenant John Hewett, Royal Marines.)

The second thing that happens is that the British fire rockets at the Americans (which have no effect except to scare them). They will fire rockets at them again at Bladensburg, Baltimore and New Orleans. If the British do not fire rockets at the Americans, then "the rockets' red glare" would never have happened, and Francis Scott Key would have needed something else to rhyme with "the bombs bursting in air" in the American national anthem.

The British Lake Ontario Navy really wants to attack Sackets Harbor again, but they don't think they're strong enough to attack it, so they attack Oswego, New York instead.

On 5 May they take 750 soldiers from Kingston armed with pikes and the war cry "Gentlemen, let us set the example!," and attack Oswego defended by only 290 Americans. The Americans abandon Oswego and the British capture 2,400 barrels of flour, salt, pork and bread, and seven cannons and ammunition;

burn the fort and other buildings; and return to Kingston. The 42 British officers then have a victory party "how they talked, how they listened, how they sang, and how they drank" (5-7 May 1814).

On 28 May the British Lake Ontario Navy is back again at Oswego. The Americans are sending 34 cannons on 19 boats from Oswego to Sackets Harbor. The British capture one boat and chase the other 18 into Sandy Creek (near Ellisburg, New York between Oswego and Sackets Harbor). The British send 200 soldiers after them but they are ambushed by American reinforcements from Sackets Harbor and all 200 are lost (196 captured, 4 killed). The British return to Kingston (28-30 May 1814). The Americans later build a road from Rome, New York to Sackets Harbor, thus eliminating the Oswego water route.

Eight hundred Americans in six ships from Erie, Pennsylvania, cross Lake Erie and raid Port Dover, Port Ryerse and Turkey Point, Ontario (14 May 1814).

With all this raiding going on in Southern Ontario, the British catch 19 traitors who have been helping the Americans and put them on trial for treason on Wilson Street in Ancaster, Ontario (18 June 1814). Fifteen are found guilty, eight are hanged and beheaded in Burlington Heights on 20 July 1814; and of the seven that are pardoned, three are banished from Canada for life, three die in jail in Kingston, and one escapes. They call it "The Ancaster Assizes."

Americans from northern New York State raid Hemmingford, Quebec across the border three times. On the first raid they capture a British spy (perhaps meeting the same fate as the eight above). On the second raid their leader is killed. And on the third raid they avenge their leader's death (28 June–10 August 1814).

The Battle of Chippawa, Ontario, 5 July 1814

At Buffalo, New York the American Army of 5,000 is under a new regime. New food, new discipline, new health standards, new training, new general. They are training 10 hours a day under their new general according to their new army training manual "Training An Army The Napoleon Bonaparte Way" by Napoleon Bonaparte, Emperor. The training includes drill, weapons handling, proper saluting, hygiene and executing deserters. By 7 June 1814 this new army is ready to invade the Niagara Peninsula again and go on to take Burlington Heights and Toronto. The only problem is the army is now down to 3,500 as 1,500 of them have either been incapacitated by the 10 hours a day training, or deserted and not been caught and executed.

Burlington Heights must seem like a mythical place to the Americans. They will march and sail towards it a number of times during this war, but never get there. They don't get there again this time either. Burlington Heights (Hamilton, Ontario) will be the most-sought-after, just-out-of-reach, never-made-it objective of the Americans during The War of 1812.

American view of Burlington Heights, Ontario during War of 1812 by an unknown artist (also available in white pine frame).

The British have been preparing for an American attack on Niagara. They feel it will come at the north end again, so they put most of their Niagara force of 2,300 in Fort Niagara (600) and Fort George (1,500). This leaves only 150 in Fort Erie and 50 in Chippawa at the south end. The American attack comes at the south end. (The British were however prepared to abandon all of Niagara and retreat to Burlington Heights once again as they had done before).

The Americans invade on 3 July and surround Fort Erie. The American general leading the attack jumps out of his boat too soon, sinks in deep water, and has to be rescued. Fort Erie fires off a few cannons and surrenders. The Americans move north towards Chippawa. The British in Chippawa (there aren't many of them) move north towards Fort George. The British in Fort George move south towards Chippawa.

By 4 July the 3,500 Americans are in Chippawa south of the Welland River, with 1,800 British north of the Welland River. The Americans withdraw south to Usshers Creek south of Chippawa, camp in the vicinity of Willick Road, Chippawa, and hold their Fourth of July celebrations (dinner and dress parade) on 5 July. However while they are celebrating the British cross the Welland River and advance towards them. The Americans suspend their one-day-late holiday and cross Usshers Creek to meet them. The two armies meet each other in the vicinity of Edgeworth Road, Chippawa.

The British Army doesn't know that this American Army has been trained according to The Napoleon Bonaparte Army Handbook. They also don't recognize them. This American Army is wearing white trousers and grey jackets instead of blue. There weren't enough of the new blue uniforms to go around, the Sackets Harbor and Plattsburgh armies took most of them, so this army makes up its own grey uniform that later becomes known as Cadet's Grey when it is adopted by the West Point Cadets (the jackets though do have extra long sleeves to allow for shrinkage).

The British attack, the Americans hold. The Americans charge, and the British retreat back across the Welland River. The losses are heavy (Americans 327 killed, wounded, missing/British 415). The British retreat north along Portage Road (it portages around Niagara Falls) all the way back to Fort George. The Americans follow them (7 July), and wait until 20 July at Queenston for The American Lake Ontario Navy from Sackets

Harbor to arrive and help them attack Fort George and Fort Niagara. But The American Lake Ontario Navy does not arrive. They stay safe and snug in Sackets Harbor building ships. So the American Army raids St. Davids and returns to Chippawa (24 July). The British follow them. They have reinforcements now from Burlington Heights and Toronto. The Americans have no reinforcements. The British are now prepared to put all their Niagara forces into one battle with the Americans. And this is what happens. It's the biggest battle of The War of 1812 in Canada (only The Battle of New Orleans is bigger).

The Battle of Lundy's Lane, Niagara Falls, Ontario, 25-26 July 1814

For one of the few times in this war the 4,000 British heading south to Niagara Falls, Ontario on the Canadian side, actually outnumber the 2,600 Americans heading north to Niagara Falls, Ontario on the Canadian side. The Americans are heading north again because 600 British from Fort Niagara are also heading south to Niagara Falls, New York on the American side, and the Americans have lots of supplies in Niagara Falls, New York (in a fort which is no longer there but used to be on the Niagara River in the south part of the city above the Falls in the vicinity of the Robert Moses Parkway west of Gill Creek).

The moon → and Johnson's Tavern ← on Lundy's Lane in the 1815 engraving "The Battle of Lundy's Lane" by William Strickland. No place for a quiet drink on the night of 25 July 1814.

The Americans find the British have taken up a position on the top of a slope in the vicinity of Lundy's Lane/Ferry Street and Portage Road/Main Street in Niagara Falls, Ontario, just north of the Falls themselves (you can hear the Falls from there). The Americans are in an open field to the south. They have the choice of either attacking or retreating. They figure that it is worse to be attacked while retreating than it is to be attacked while attacking, so they attack. It is 7:15 p.m. on 26 July 1814, and neither side knows how strong the other side is.

The British stop the first American charge, but the Americans outflank the British along Portage Road and capture a wounded British general when his stretcher bearers carry him by mistake into the American lines not the British lines. It's getting dark. The British re-form and hold the top of the slope where their six cannons are. It's now 9:00 p.m. and getting really dark. Reinforcements are pushed up to the front lines of both sides. There is a "short intermission" during which soldiers drink water from canteens and munch on dry biscuits (there is no popcorn or soft drinks available).

The Americans gain the top of the slope by a combination of darkness and hiding in the shrubbery, and capture the British cannons. Another British general is wounded. The Americans bring their three cannons to the top of the slope too. The British attack the top of the slope to try to get their cannons back. Lundy's Lane at the top of the slope is a popular place where everybody wants to be. It's now midnight and completely confusing. British shoot at Americans and other British. Americans shoot at British and other Americans. From a distance of 15 yards who can tell who is who in the pitch black? The British make three attempts to regain the top of the slope, but fail. Then the Americans are ordered off the top of the slope. They are tired and running out of ammunition and water. When they leave the British retake the top of the slope and recapture all their cannons and two of the American cannons. But they are too tired and disorganized as well to chase after the Americans. The Battle of Lundy's Lane is over. The losses are about equal: 1,737 killed, wounded and missing (American 861, British 876).

The Lundy's Lane memorial 1895
Niagara Falls, Ontario

On the morning of 26 July the Americans return to retake Lundy's Lane, but find the British have reformed their defences and reinforced the top of the slope. So they turn around and head back south. The British let them go.

The Americans burn the bridge over the Welland River at Chippawa, throw their heavy baggage into the Niagara River (where it goes over Niagara Falls), and go back to Fort Erie. The British do not follow them. At least not right away. They go back to Queenston and reorganize. In the meantime the Americans bring over 2,200 reinforcements from Sackets Harbor (the ones with the new blue uniforms), and start rebuilding Fort Erie. When the British are sufficiently reorganized they camp outside Fort Erie and wait for their heavy cannons to arrive from Fort George (3 August). The Siege of Fort Erie has begun.

The American Lake Ontario Navy arrives off Niagara on 5 August. Almost four weeks late. The American army expected them on 10 July. They blockade Fort George, Fort Niagara and Kingston to stop any supplies reaching Niagara, but it's too late. The American Army is not poised to attack Fort George and Fort Niagara and go on to take Burlington Heights and Toronto. They are now 30 miles south in Fort Erie and under siege by the British.

Around the time of The Battle of Chippawa and the Battle of Lundy's Lane, there are a series of two completely unrelated events that take place quite a bit north and west of Niagara (but not as far west as Astoria, Oregon). And they both have to do with little Mackinac Island in Northern Michigan that the British captured early in the war and have held ever since. The Americans want Mackinac Island back. And they want Prairie du Chien, Wisconsin back too while they're at it.

Prairie du Chien, Wisconsin, 17-10 July 1814

Prairie du Chien, Wisconsin is a much more important place in 1814 than it is now. Prairie du Chien, Wisconsin is at the corner of the Mississippi River and the Wisconsin River, and that makes it important. The French build a trading post and fort there in 1673. The British do the same in 1685. In 1783 The United States builds a fort there. In 1813 they come back and rebuild it. In early 1814 the British capture it. In May 1814 the Americans send 130 Indians, 16 "Michigan Fencibles" and one cannon up the Mississippi River from St. Louis, Missouri to take it back, which they do, just by showing up.

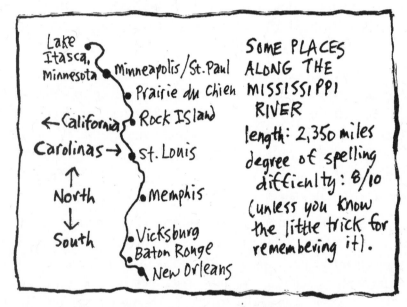

The British on Macinac Island, 350 miles away, don't like that. Prairie due Chien is in their backyard. Their area of jurisdiction. And so on 28 June they send 63 "Mississippi Volunteers" to take it back again. They travel into Lake Michigan, down Green Bay to the Fox River, up the Fox River to Portage, Wisconsin, and down the Wisconsin River to Prairie du Chien, picking up Indians and the former Prairie du Chien British garrison as they go, and arriving on 17 July with a force of 650. The Americans are busy rebuilding the fort and are caught by surprise. After a siege of three days the 66 men, 61 muskets, 46 barrels of flour, 20 barrels of pork, five cannons, one woman and one child inside the fort, surrender. Prairie du Chien is a fort of two blockhouses with a stockade around it. The British build another blockhouse.

The Americans try to recapture Prairie du Chien again from St. Louis, but are ambushed by the British at Rock Island, Illinois on the Mississippi and retreat back to St. Louis. In August they try again, sending 350 in eight boats up the Mississippi, but are stopped again at Rock Island by 30 British and 1,000 Indians (5 September). They retreat back down the river to Keokuk, Iowa for a bit, and then back to St. Louis in October. The British keep Prairie du Chien until the end of the war, when under The Treaty of Ghent it is handed back to the Americans in a burned and abandoned state. Rock Island, Illinois keeps its reputation as the ideal Mississippi River ambush spot until 1954 when Huddie Ledbetter writes a railway song about it (*"The Rock Island Line"*), its ambush days are quickly forgotten, and it becomes a railway and hit parade town instead.

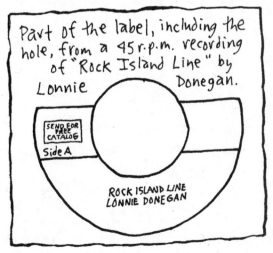

Part of the label, including the hole, from a 45 r.p.m. recording of "Rock Island Line" by Lonnie Donegan.

SEND FOR FREE CATALOG

Side A

ROCK ISLAND LINE
LONNIE DONEGAN

The American Attack on Mackinac Island, Michigan, 3 July – 5 August 1814

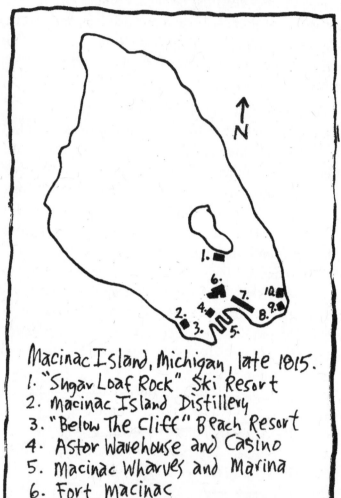

Macinac Island, Michigan, late 1815.
1. "Sugar Loaf Rock" Ski Resort
2. Macinac Island Distillery
3. "Below The Cliff" Beach Resort
4. Astor Warehouse and Casino
5. Macinac Wharves and Marina
6. Fort Macinac
7. Macinac Entertainment Strip
8. Macinac Time-Share Condominium Resort
9. Macinac Island Brewery
10. Macinac Island Winery

The British expect the Americans to try to recapture Mackinac Island, so during the winter of 1813-14 they send reinforcements for Mackinac from Kingston to Toronto, then overland to Lake Simcoe, then down the Nottawasaga River to Georgian Bay, arriving at Mackinac on 18 May. One month later Mackinac sends the 63 volunteers away to recapture Prairie du Chien. The 500 British and two cannons left on Mackinac Island, build a blockhouse on the high ground above the fort that caused problems for the defence of the fort in the past, and wait for the Americans. They don't have too long to wait.

On 3 July, 750 Americans in five ships sail north from Detroit to recapture Mackinac. Along the way they burn the British fort on St. Joseph's Island (it's deserted, when the British left St. Joseph's Island for Mackinac they never went back), and the dockyard at Sault Ste. Marie, Ontario (21 July, it's not deserted); arriving off Mackinac on 26 July. They find however that they can't elevate the cannons on their ships high enough to shoot at the fort, so they decide to land at the north end of the island and attack the fort from the rear as the British did to them in 1812. But the British know the Americans are going to do this, and they hide in the woods at the north end of the island and ambush them, and the Americans retreat back to their ships (4 August). The next day the Americans leave two ships behind to blockade Mackinac and the other three ships sail away. On their way back to Detroit they find and destroy the only British ship on the Upper Lakes hiding in the Nottawasaga River at Wasaga Beach, Ontario (13 August).

On 2 September the British in rowboats and canoes capture one of the two blockading American ships in the North Channel of Georgian Bay near Thessalon, Ontario; and four days later they capture the second ship with the first ship. Mackinac Island is held by the British until the end of the war when it too, like Prairie du Chien, is handed back to the Americans.

The Siege of Fort Erie, Ontario,
3 August – 5 November 1814

The Niagara Peninsula of Ontario was the site of the first major American invasion and battle in The War of 1812. It's also the site of the last. The first was at Queenston Heights at the north end of the Niagara River. The last is at Fort Erie at the south end.

The Americans go back to Fort Erie after The Battle of Lundy's Lane. The British don't arrive until 3 August. And so begins The Siege of Fort Erie. By that time there are 3,000 Americans and 16 cannons inside Fort Erie, and 3,000 British and six cannons outside Fort Erie, and Fort Erie itself is in the best shape it has ever been in in its life. Fort Erie has had a tough time of it during The War of 1812. Abandoned, surrendered, burned, blown up, wrecked, never properly finished, never properly attacked, and never properly defended. This upcoming action though, the last drawn out battle of the war in Canada, and the last offensive action of The United States in the war, is Fort Erie's big moment. Before that Fort Erie was a place that the war passed in and out of and went by without much of a fuss. But now Fort Erie is the centre of attention. The end of the war in Canada belongs to Fort Erie. At the end of the Niagara Peninsula. At the end of Canada.

The Americans rebuild and redesign Fort Erie. The original fort is left in the north corner and a new fort is built up around it. There are now gun batteries at each end, a seven foot high earth wall in between, a ditch in front, a palisade wall (wall of logs with pointy ends pointing up), and an abattis (line of tree branches with pointy ends pointing out).

The British build the first fort at Fort Erie in 1764. The first of three forts. The first fort is built too close to the lake and is wrecked by a storm. The second fort is moved back a bit from the lake, but is also wrecked by a storm. So after two wrecked forts in 39 years the British finally realize that Lake Erie is no quiet mill pond to build a fort beside, but a lake

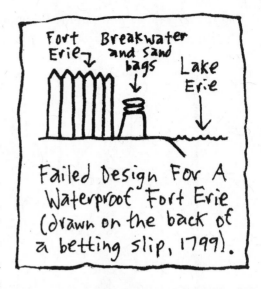

Failed Design For A Waterproof Fort Erie (drawn on the back of a betting slip, 1799).

bigger than Wales, the state of Massachusetts, or four-and-a-half provinces of Prince Edward Island, with storms on it that can wreck forts. What they didn't know was that Lake Erie is a relatively shallow lake as far as big lakes go, and so particularly able to whip up fort-wrecking storms.

So in 1803 they begin building a third Fort Erie on higher ground back from the shore, and using stone instead of wood. It's planned to have four bastions, a two-storey barracks, a moat, officers' quarters, guardhouse, powder magazine and storehouses. Three years after starting construction only two of the bastions, the barracks and the moat are completed, and work has stopped. When The War of 1812 comes along Fort Erie is still unfinished. During the war it changes hands four times, and three times the side abandoning it blows it up and wrecks it before they leave.

The British re-occupy Fort Erie after the war, partially rebuild it again, and then abandon it again in 1823 for the next 78 years. It is protected from crumbling further into decay in 1901, and restoration begins in 1937. But although Fort Erie is a British fort, it is rebuilt to the star-shaped, 38-inch-thick stone-walled fort that the Americans built in the five months they occupied it during The War of 1812. The fort the British now face on 3 August 1814.

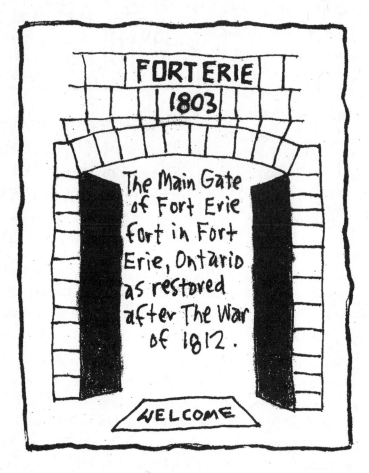

The Main Gate of Fort Erie fort in Fort Erie, Ontario as restored after The War of 1812.

When the British arrive at Fort Erie they camp one-and-a-half miles north of the fort (near The Fort Erie Race Track), and send 600 soldiers across the river to attack Buffalo, New York, the supply link to the Americans inside Fort Erie. This is a complete failure. "Without possessing one solitary excuse" they return without attacking "an unpardonable degree of unsteadiness" (240 Americans ambushed them).

The British begin firing their cannons at Fort Erie on 13 August. This is also a complete failure ("the cannons were not adequate"). So the British plan a surprise, three-pronged, sneak, night attack on the fort for 15 August. Again, as at Lundy's Lane, neither side knows how strong the other side is. The British think there are 1,500 Americans inside the fort, and the Americans think there are 5,000 British outside.

At 2 a.m. the main attack, the south prong (1,300), attacks the south end of the fort. They get stuck in the abattis. There aren't enough ladders to get over the walls, and the ladders aren't tall enough. They get lost in the dark. They go into the lake to get around the defences, and are shot at in the water. The Americans are waiting for them. They are stopped, retreat, and many are captured.

The centre prong (250) and the north prong (650) are to attack when the south prong has successfully attacked. But the south prong has not successfully attacked. The centre prong and the north prong get lost in the dark too, miss their attacking targets, and end up together as one prong. They attack three times, two commanding officers are killed, but on the fourth attempt they break into one of the bastions, capture an American cannon, fire it into the fort, hit the powder magazine, and blow themselves and some Americans up. Only a few escape. The north and centre prongs retreat too. The British lose 316 killed or wounded, 539 missing (prisoners or deserted); the Americans 84 killed or wounded.

The British retreat north. It rains a lot ("a lake in the midst of a thick wood"). The weather gets worse. The soldiers sleep on logs. They bring in 1,200 reinforcements and move closer again to the fort. The Americans bring in more reinforcements too, and on 17 September in a surprise, sneak, night attack of their own, they attack the British cannon located south of Garrison Road, Fort Erie, capturing two and destroying a third in the vicinity of The

Country Fair Mall. (British: 115 killed, 178 wounded, 316 missing/Americans: 79 killed, 432 wounded or missing. The two battles at Fort Erie together are bigger than Lundy's Lane). Faced with sickness and rain for 13 straight days, and unsuccessful in retaking Fort Erie, the British withdraw further north to Chippawa on 21 September.

The Americans bring in 3,500 more reinforcements from Plattsburgh to join the 2,800 already in Fort Erie, and on 13 October they follow the British north to Usshers Creek where they had been earlier in the year at The Battle of Chippawa. Then, despite having the largest army they have ever had to invade Canada with, they burn 200 bushels of wheat at a mill in Welland, Ontario (19 October), return to Fort Erie, blow it up, and return to Buffalo (1 November), where the American commander complains about "this inclement climate" and resigns.

Hats of The War of 1812.

#6. The Sackets Harbor "Sailor Boys" Watchcap. (one size fits all)

Four days later Captain James FitzGibbon (the same fellow Laura Secord walked to see and the hero of The Battle of Beaver Dams), goes to have a peek at Fort Erie to see what is going on, and finds it deserted. The Americans have gone and the British didn't even know they'd left.

And so ends the American invasion part of The War of 1812. Beaten by the Canadian weather. From now on until The Treaty of Ghent is signed on 24 December, The War of 1812 will be a purely defensive war for the Americans (except for the raids into Southern Ontario in October 1814), and it will be the British that will do all the invading.

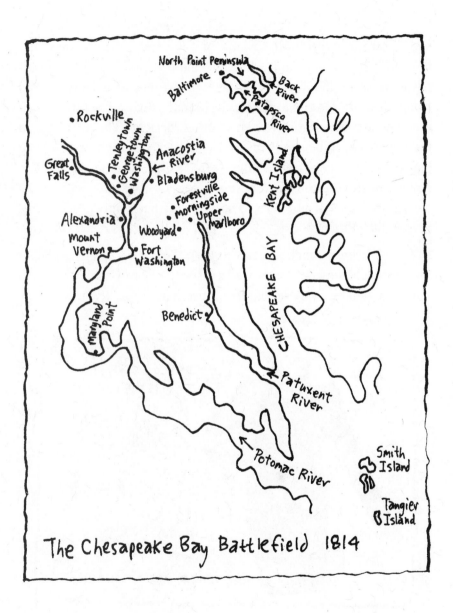

The Chesapeake Bay Battlefield 1814

The Battle of Bladensburg, Maryland, 24 August 1814

In April 1814 France is defeated and Napoleon abdicates and is sent to exile on the island of Elba (not much of an exile, he's only 35 miles from his home island of Corsica and 150 miles from France). The war in Europe is over (until Napoleon escapes from Elba and returns to France in March 1815). The British can now concentrate on the war in North America. They will go on the offensive. They will raid the American east coast to create havoc, retake northern Maine lost to the Americans in The American Revolutionary War, take New Orleans and control the Mississippi River, and force The United States into peace terms favourable to them.

"I have it much at heart to give them a complete drubbing before peace is made," says the British naval commander in North America. And so they set out to do just that.

A British fleet with 4,000 soldiers leaves Bordeaux, France on 2 June 1814, reaches Bermuda on 25 July, enters Chesapeake Bay on 16 August, and makes Tangier Island, Virginia its base. The idea of attacking Washington, D.C. is appealing. The main target of this campaign is supposed to be Baltimore, Maryland, but the British decide to make a lightning strike on Washington D.C. first, just for the fun of it, and because they're in the neighbourhood and passing by anyway (and because the year before they learned that Washington was poorly defended).

The Americans argue about who should be in charge of the defence of Washington, and even if Washington will be attacked. Under the newly-organized American military structure (2 July 1814), Washington D.C. is in the Tenth Military District under a Tenth Military District Commander who reports to the Secretary of War who reports to the Secretary of State who reports to the President. The newly-appointed Tenth Military District Commander, who also has to defend Baltimore, is one of those generals captured at The Battle of Stoney Creek. Not a good omen.

The Tenth Military District Commander argues with the Washington Militia Commander over who should command the militia. A decision on the situation is passed to the Secretary of War and then to the President. The Washington Militia Commander resigns. The Secretary of War doesn't think Washington will be attacked. The Tenth Military District Commander thinks Washington will be attacked, and he rides up and down the Potomac River shoreline trying to figure out where the British might land, while at the same time trying to reassure everybody that they won't land and won't attack. But there are too many places where the British might land and attack from. They could come up the Potomac. Or they could come up the Chesapeake. They come up both. And they also come up the

Patuxent River too. And they land. And they have every intention of attacking as well.

The British plan a two-pronged attack on Washington. A southern naval attack, and a northeastern overland infantry attack. The north prong sails up the Patuxent River, lands at Benedict, Maryland (19 August, it is deserted in anticipation of their arrival), and begins marching north to Upper Marlboro, Maryland (it's almost deserted too except for Dr. William Beanes, a friend of Francis Scott Key's). The weather is very warm ("the hottest summer in memory"). Sixty British soldiers in heavy woolen winter uniforms will die of heatstroke marching around Maryland in 100° F heat. Having met no resistance so far, it is at Upper Marlboro that the British decide to definitely go ahead and attack Washington.

Washington is protected by Fort Washington, Maryland, 12 miles south of the city on the Potomac River, a well-constructed fort but manned by a force of only 80 which permits only five of its 27 cannons to be fired; a local militia of 15,000 most of whom exist only on paper; and 1,120 poorly trained, poorly equipped and poorly organized soldiers stationed around the city.

Washington has no warning of the advancing British until 18 August. They call up the militia; urge them to take all broken or faulty weapons to designated shops for repair; ride off to scout the British without taking a telescope; react to false alarms and rumours; accidently shoot at each other; march to and fro to contradictory orders; scuttle boats in Chesapeake Bay; destroy two bridges leading into Washington; send ammunition and artillery out of the city for safekeeping; commandeer wagons to remove government papers (there aren't enough of them as everybody else is abandoning Washington too); bring the Baltimore Militia to Bladensburg, Maryland with no training, no uniforms, 80% faulty weapons, and a commander whose best military attribute is a loud voice (5,000 of them arrive just in time for The Battle of

Bladensburg); and send 2,000 Washington Militia out of the city where they see the advancing British near Morningside, Maryland and retreat to Forestville, Maryland where they join up with the outlying militia retreating from Woodyard, Maryland (20 August).

The British leave Upper Marlboro on 23 August and head for Bladensburg where there is a bridge over the Anacostia River (east branch of the Potomac, the bridges closer to Washington over the Potomac and the Anacostia having been destroyed by the Americans). The Americans have gathered 7,000 tired and hungry defenders into two lines on the top of a hill on the west side of the river across from the Bladensburg bridge, including 113 marines manning cannons in a fortified house. They are still arguing over who is in command.

The British approach Bladensburg from the east side of the river on 24 August. They are also tired and hungry after a seven hour march. They fire off rockets (the ones with the red glare), and charge across the bridge and the river. There is some resistance and then the two American lines run away down the Bladensburg Road, some to Washington, some to Georgetown, and some to Tenleytown (they also call this battle "The Bladensburg Races"). "Never did men with arms in their hands make better use of their legs." They even outrun the fleeing civilians who have come out from Washington to watch the battle (one of whom is Francis Scott Key). Only the marines make a stand of it, and then they too run. The British do not go after them. "The victors were too weary and the vanquished too swift." (Americans: 12 killed, 40 wounded/British 64 killed, 185 wounded).

The burning of Washington D.C., 24-25 August 1814

The British southern naval attack on Washington of six ships and 1,000 soldiers, goes up the Potomac River arriving at Maryland Point, Maryland on the same day as The Battle of Bladensburg (24 August). They sail past George Washington's house at Mount Vernon, Virginia (blowing raspberries at it and otherwise showing no reverence whatsoever for this national historic site), and bombard Fort Washington, miss, but watch the Americans blow up the powder magazine and abandon the fort for them (27 August, another exploding powder magazine, the American commander is later dismissed from the army). The British then bombard Fort Washington from close range, land, and wreck what they can of the rest of it (they are though impressed by how well built and designed it is). They then sail farther up the river and raid Alexandria, Virginia (28 August – 3 September), capturing 21 ships, 16,000 barrels of flour, 1,000 barrels of tobacco, 150 bales of cotton, and $5,000 worth of other goods; and then sail back down the river. The Americans ambush them in the Potomac River near Mount Vernon, Virginia and Indian Head, Maryland, but the British escape (7 September).

After The Battle of Bladensburg the British land attack rests for two hours and then begins marching into Washington at 6 p.m., arriving that night. Ahead of them the Americans burn the navy yard, two ships and five smaller boats, and decide to "fall back on the Capitol and there form for battle." Then they decide to retreat west along Pennsylvania Avenue to Georgetown. Then three miles farther north up Wisconsin Avenue to Tenleytown. Then after three hours rest another five miles west along the River Road, and then another seven miles north to Rockville, Maryland. The American government retreats even farther, 50 miles northwest up the River Road to Frederick, Maryland, then across the Potomac River and farther west into Virginia. The President rides all the way to Great Falls, Virginia on horseback.

When the main body of the British Army enters Washington lots of it is already on fire, small units of skilled arsonists having already been sent ahead into the city to burn selected sites. The city is almost deserted. Washington D.C. in 1814 has a population of 8,000, three street lamps, pot-holed roads, and mosquito-infested swamps. They are still chopping down trees to make the streets according to the plan approved by George Washington (Washington forecast that the city "would be a metropolis by 1800"). The President's House is near a swamp and is still not finished (begun in 1792). It has 23 rooms, no indoor toilets, no water supply, a leaky roof and rotted floorboards. The Capitol Building is in "a deep morass covered with alder bushes." The government has only been in Washington for 14 years (before that it led a rather nomadic existence). Many government employees prefer to live three miles away west in Georgetown.

The sort of dress with plunging neckline and small, tight, wrap-around necklace worn by 36 year old Dolley Madison in the famous 1804 painting of her by Gilbert Stuart.

The British march down Maryland Avenue to Capitol Square, and then down Pennsylvania Avenue to burn the Treasury Building; the Capitol Building; the barracks; the arsenal (where 30 British soldiers accidently blow themselves up); and the President's House, but not before British officers eat the meal and drink the wine already prepared and set out for 40 guests to celebrate the American victory at Bladensburg, and after Mrs. Dolley Madison, the President's wife, has rescued the George Washington painting by Gilbert Stuart from the house. (This is the "Lansdowne" painting of 1796, the full-length portrait of Washington standing beside his writing table, quill pen in inkwell, with his right hand extended and his left hand on his sword, dressed in a one-piece, wrist-to-knee length dark smock with long dark stockings and buckle shoes. Stuart also did the "Athenaeum" painting of 1796, probably the best known head and shoulders portrait of Washington. Stuart could apparently knock off a copy of his own portraits at the rate of one every two hours. In return the British take Dolley Madison's portrait and the President's dress sword).

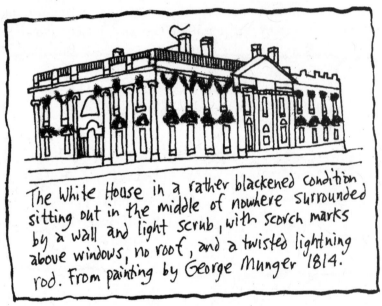

The White House in a rather blackened condition, sitting out in the middle of nowhere surrounded by a wall and light scrub, with scorch marks above windows, no roof, and a twisted lightning rod. From painting by George Munger 1814.

The British then camp for the night in the Library of Congress block in the vicinity of 1st Street and East Capitol Street. On 25 August they burn the State and War Departments, wreck a newspaper office and a rope works, and then after "the awfullest storms which raged for a long time," begin marching back out of the city the way they'd come in (at the same time as the southern naval attack is looting Alexandria, Virginia), and by 29 August they are back in their ships again at Benedict, Maryland.

After the British leave Washington and before the government returns and some semblance of law and order is restored, looters rampage through the city. The President returns on 28 August (via Brookeville, Maryland), and goes to live on F Street North. The Capitol Building and the President's House are scorched walls only, no roof. They are both rebuilt and the President's House is painted white to cover the burn marks. (It was the only colour of paint available, black would have done the job better and the President's wife expressed a preference for lavender, and so but for paint availability the "White House" could have been called the "Lavender House." It was apparently known as The White House before 1814 anyway). The American Secretary of War resigns, and the Tenth Military District Commander is court-martialled.

The two British fleets from the Potomac and the Patuxent meet up in the Chesapeake, and after some discussion decide to head north and attack Baltimore after all. But before they get there the British launch two other attacks farther north on places that are much more important to them than either Washington or Baltimore: Maine and Plattsburgh, New York.

The Conquering of Maine (or "The Penobscot Expedition"). 21 June – 18 September 1814

In terms of the overall British plans for The War of 1812 in the year of 1814, Maine was one of the most important objectives, certainly more important than Washington or Baltimore. The British want to retake that part of northern Maine down to the Penobscot River that they lost after The American Revolutionary War. Maine was valuable to the British. Maine had pine forests full of great pine trees for ships' masts. Maine had great harbours, especially Penobscot Bay. Maine was too close to New Brunswick for comfort.

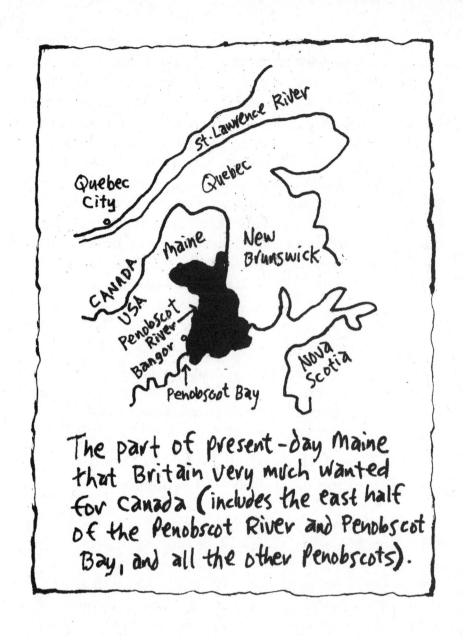

The part of present-day Maine that Britain very much wanted for Canada (includes the east half of the Penobscot River and Penobscot Bay, and all the other Penobscots).

And Maine stuck up too close into Quebec for comfort too (during The American Revolutionary War the Americans came up through northern Maine to attack Quebec City in 1775). Maine was just too darn close to Canada for comfort. So the British plan

to conquer Maine, force the Americans into peace terms favourable to them, and annex northern Maine into Canada. The attack
on Washington and the attacks on Baltimore and Plattsburgh to
come, are just diversionary tactics designed to soften up the
Americans in order to take Maine. Maine is the big prize. The
British really like Maine. Especially Penobscot Bay (they really
liked it during The American Revolutionary war too, taking
Castine, Maine in Penobscot Bay in June 1779 and holding it for
the rest of the war until forced to give it back, reluctantly only
because they'd lost the war). They like it in The War of 1812 too.
In fact they like it so much they call the conquering of Maine "The
Penobscot Expedition." Perhaps never before, or since, has
anyone coveted northern Maine so much or shown it such careful,
detailed planning and attention. The British really like Penobscot
Bay. And they really like saying Penobscot too. Penobscot is a
really fun word to say.

Hats of The
War of 1812.

#7. The Baltimore
"Orioles" militia.

The Penobscot Expedition
begins on 21 June 1814 when the
British raid Thomaston and Saint
George, Maine (west side of
Penobscot Bay). Then the 336
Americans and six cannons
defending Eastport, Maine (east
Maine near New Brunswick),
surrender to 600 British on 11 July.
The British now control Penobscot
Bay and Passamaquoddy Bay.
(Even if they have difficulty
spelling Passamaquoddy they still
enjoy saying it too along with
Penobscot. Both Passamaquoddy and Penobscot are fun words to
say (see Appendix: "Fun Words To Say From The War of 1812").

British Plans For Penobscot and Castine Settlements in Maine, 1814.
note: Only five of these towns exist today.

Penobscot River and to Penobscot County

Penobscot Bay

Northwest Penobscot

North Penobscot

West Penobscot

Central Penobscot

East Penobscot

Far West Penobscot

Penobscot

Penobscot Penobscot

Southwest Penobscot

Penobscot Bay/et

South Penobscot

Deep Southwest Penobscot

Deep South Penobscot

Fort George
Castine

Map Drawn By: Captain P. Penobscot, Royal Navy Drafting Corps., Penobscot House, Penobscot Lane, Chatham, U.K. 1814.

It is now time for the Penobscot part of The Penobscot Expedition. On 21 August The Penobscot Expeditionary Force of 21 ships and 2,500 troops sails from Halifax, Nova Scotia into Penobscot Bay, approaching Castine, Maine on 1 September. The American defenders fire one cannon volley and then abandon Castine retreating north up the Penobscot River. The British follow them. They take Belfast, Maine; then Bucksport, Maine; then Frankfort, Maine; then Hampden, Maine (2 September), where there is a battle in thick fog against 1,400 American militia. Both sides shoot at each other by sound rather than sight. The British fire rockets and the Americans retreat farther north, setting

fire to a ship and abandoning 20 cannons. The British then take
Bangor, Maine, stop, eat Bangor's fresh meat and bread and drink
Bangor's fine wine and liquor, and then return to Castine as
triumphant conquerers of the lower part of the Penobscot River
and masters of Penobscot Bay (9 September). Along the way they
have given every American one week to take the oath of allegiance
to the King or leave. (Two-thirds accept. What choice do they
have? Who will help them in northern Maine? And besides they
didn't want the war in the first place, the people of Nova Scotia
and New Brunswick are their close friends, certainly closer than
New York or Washington anyway).

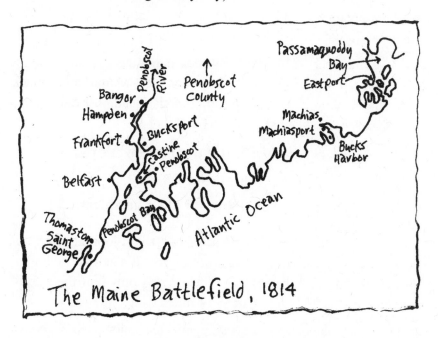

The Maine Battlefield, 1814

The next phase of The Penobscot Expedition is to control
everything between Penobscot Bay and Eastport (there isn't
much). The British land 900 soldiers at Bucks Harbor, Maine,
(south of Machias in Machias Bay), and march north to
Machiasport, Maine, which they burn. By the time they get to
Machias, Maine, their objective, Machias has been abandoned in

anticipation of their arrival. The British are now in possession of Northern Maine (18 September). It feels pretty good. The British have been looking forward to this since 1783. Half of The Penobscot Expeditionary Force returns to Halifax (reluctantly), and the other half (the lucky ones), get to stay on and occupy Northern Maine. Fort George at Castine (another Fort George but as this one is 500 miles east of the Fort George at Niagara, not likely to get mixed up with any of the other Fort Georges either), is rebuilt and outfitted with 60 cannons, such is the British Army's affection for Castine, Maine. The British really do like Castine, Maine in Penobscot Bay (Penobscot is voted one of the funnest words to say in the whole of The War of 1812, just as it was in The American Revolutionary War 35 years ago.

September 1814 is a busy month for the British. Within the space of several weeks they conquer Maine and attack Plattsburgh, New York and Baltimore, Maryland. Plattsburgh is next. Maine was successful. Plattsburgh is not.

The Battle of Plattsburgh, New York, 11 September 1814
(Also called The Battle of Lake Champlain)

Lake Champlain is a small lake. If you look at a map of North America you won't even notice it. It's not on a list of "Principal Natural Lakes of the World." It's only half the size of Luxembourg and only one-half to 14 miles wide.

(1) In an independent survey conducted amongst prospective overseas British settlers, most said they preferred to go somewhere named Penobscot, be it Penobscot Bay, the Penobscot River, Penobscot County, or Penobscot town. Castine, Maine came second.

(2) But Lake Champlain does have one thing going for it. It's 125 miles long, and if you follow it from south to north it flows directly from New York State into Canada and down the Richelieu River to Sorel, Quebec on the St. Lawrence River. And in 1814, and before 1814, that was important. If you wanted to invade Canada you could use this water route north. The Americans did it in The American Revolutionary War (1775), and tried to do it several times in the War of 1812 (Lacolle, Quebec). Likewise if you wanted to invade the United States you could use this water route south. The British tried to do it in The American Revolutionary War (Saratoga, 1777) and now they will try to do it again in 1814.

The trouble with Lake Champlain however is that it's dead-ended at its southern end near Whitehall, New York. If you want to go north you have to bring everything you need overland to the lake, or build it on the lake. If you want to go south, you can only go as far as Whitehall, New York. You then have to portage over 15 miles to the Hudson River. Or, you can portage at Fort Ticonderoga over to Lake George, go up Lake George, and then have a shorter 10 mile portage to the Hudson. Either way it's not simple (today there's The Champlain Canal to connect the lake to the Hudson). But in 1814 Lake Champlain was thought to be quite important (more important than it really was).

And so like Lake Erie and Lake Ontario, Lake Champlain has its own War of 1812 navies and its own War of 1812 naval battle too, just on a smaller scale (Lake Champlain is seven times larger than The District of Columbia, more than twice the size of The Isle of Man, and about four-and-a-half times smaller that Prince Edward Island). As Canada has very little of Lake Champlain, its main port is Île-aux-Noix, Quebec on the Richelieu River. As The United States has most of Lake Champlain, its main ports are Burlington, Vermont on the east side of the lake (the biggest town on the lake), and Plattsburgh, New York on the west side of the lake ("a grand wealthy village" straddling the Saranac River).

In 1812 neither side has any navy on Lake Champlain. In 1813 the British have three oar-propelled gunboats, but the Americans have two gunboats and two ships. The Americans then sail their two ships down the Richelieu River, get trapped by the British, can't turn around, and are captured. The British now have two ships on Lake Champlain and the Americans have none. The British rename the two American ships and then attack Lake Champlain with them. They attack Chazy, Cumberland Bay and Plattsburgh, New York on the west side of the lake; and Swanton, Burlington, Shelburne, Charlotte and Kingsland Bay, Vermont on the east side; capture a few vessels and supplies, and return to I'lle-aux-Noix.

The Americans shift their Lake Champlain naval yard south from Burlington, Vermont to Vergennes, Vermont, and build three new ships. They also capture six spars being towed down the Lake by the British to be used on ships being built at I'lle-aux-Noix. They keep a look out for main masts also being towed down the lake for these ships, but see none. The Americans now have three ships on Lake Champlain, and the British have two. But the British build two more ships at I'lle-aux-Noix, so the Americans build another one at Vergennes in 50 days.

By 1814 both sides now have a navy of four big ships. The British ships are called *Confiance*, *Linnet*, *Finch*, and *Chubb*; all fine upstanding names. The American ships are called *Saratoga*, *Eagle*, *Ticonderoga*, and *Preble* all fine patriotic names except *Preble*. But the British also have an army of 10,351 ready to attack Plattsburgh with (the largest British army ever assembled in The War of 1812, two-thirds of which are veterans of the Duke of Wellington's army which defeated Napoleon in Spain); and the Americans have only 3,300 to defend Plattsburgh with (they had 4,000 more but sent them off to Sackets Harbor to attack Niagara).

On 31 August the British Army leaves Quebec City. They cross the border on their way to Plattsburgh stopping at Champlain, New York (3 September, headquarters at Judge Moore's house); Chazy, New York (4 September, headquarters at the Chazy Public Library and Alexander Scott's house); Ingraham, New York (5 September, headquarters at Sampson's Tavern); and Beekmantown, New York (6 September, headquarters at the Farnsworth Tavern and Ira Howe's house), where there is a small skirmish on Culver Hill (south of East Beekmantown which is itself south and east of Beekmantown). By 6 September they are on the north side of Plattsburgh and the Saranac River.

The British army is big, but it is not very together. The commander thinks uniforms are important ("the established uniform of the corps"). The veteran soldiers couldn't care less about uniforms ("we might be rigged out in all the colours of the rainbow if we fancied it"). The commander has a plan to take Plattsburgh. The soldiers don't think much of the plan ("there were neither Guides, Spies or Plans").

The Americans are defending Plattsburgh on the south side of the river with three forts, two blockhouses, two torn down bridges, and lots of supplies. The American Lake Champlain Navy (four big ships and nine little ones), is in Plattsburgh Bay. Instead of attacking Plattsburgh the British Army waits. They wait for their cannons to be set up, and they wait for the British Lake Champlain Navy to arrive (four big ships and 11 little ones).

On 9 September the Americans make a surprise, sneak night attack and destroy some of the British cannons. On 10 September the British Lake Champlain Navy arrives. And on 11 September the attack on Plattsburgh begins. It's a three-pronged attack. The British Lake Champlain Navy will attack the American Lake Champlain Navy at the same time as part of the British Army crosses over the river and sneaks around to attack Plattsburgh from the rear, and the other part of the British Army attacks Plattsburgh head-on. Plattsburgh shouldn't have much of a chance to survive this overwhelming three-pronged onslaught. But it doesn't turn out like that. It turns out that the fortunes of The Battle of Plattsburgh depend entirely upon the battle between the two navies.

The British Lake Champlain Navy sails into Plattsburgh Bay at 7:00 a.m. on 11 September 1814, and attacks the American Lake Champlain Navy at 8:30 a.m. By 10:50 a.m. the battle is over and the British Lake Champlain Navy is totally defeated. *Finch* goes aground, *Chubb* drifts and is captured, *Confiance* and *Linnet* surrender, and the British captain is killed.

The Naval Battle of Plattsburgh
11 September 1814
4 big ships and 11 little ones
VRS.
4 big ships and 9 little ones
(the 13 beat the 15)

Back on land, the sneaking-around-to-the-rear attack of the British Army are having a late breakfast and are not told to get going until 10:00 a.m., when the naval battle is well underway and almost over. They get lost. By the time they reach the other side of the river the naval battle is over. The head-on attack attacks head-on, is stopped, and is then called off when they see that the British Navy has lost. The sneaking-around-to-the-rear attack, which by now has snuck around to the rear and is attacking, and doing a very good job of it too, and thinks that they could just carry on attacking and take Plattsburgh all by themselves in 20 minutes or so if you wanted them to; is also called off, even though they didn't want to be called off and saw no reason why they should be called off. By 9:00 p.m. that night, in the pouring rain, the British Army is retreating back north. They have lost more soldiers from desertion than they have in battle, and they have hardly had a battle (British: 35 killed, 47 wounded, 72 prisoners, 234 missing/Americans: 37 killed, 62 wounded).

The Americans have another naval hero: Master Commandant Thomas Macdonough, who for all his success at Plattsburgh is promoted to Captain, which doesn't even sound as impressive as being a Master Commandant (he does though also have a monument at Plattsburgh).

The British commander at Plattsburgh, Lord George Prevost, who previously had done such a good job organizing the defence of Canada since 1812, is ordered to return to Britain late in 1814 to face a court-martial on the defeat at Plattsburgh.

The Battle of Baltimore, Maryland,
12-14 September 1814

As one British army is retreating from Plattsburgh, the other British army that had walked into Washington is preparing to bombard Baltimore. When Washington is being attacked Baltimore is equally as poorly defended. But rather than resigning itself to a poor military showing as at Blandensburg, or abandoning ship as Washington had done, Baltimore decides to defend itself. And so the British find that Baltimore is much better defended than Washington was. For one thing they don't have the Tenth Military District Commander in charge, they have their own Committee of Vigilance and Safety under their own commander Major General

Samuel Smith who had fought in The American Revolutionary War. And The Committee of Vigilance and Safety vigilantly plans in committees to keep Baltimore safe.

From a population of 45,000 Baltimore recruits 15,500 volunteer militia (many from outside the city and outside the state), including 9,000 along Russell Street ("The Russell Street Repellers"); 1,000 and 57 cannons in Fort McHenry (a five-pointed star fort of stone and dirt designed by the French and guarding Baltimore harbour); 80 and 6 cannons in Fort Covington west of Fort McHenry on Locust Point; and 1,400 in out-lying areas ("The Baltimore Suburban Defence League").

They organize work brigades, hospitals, bank loans and family relief; jail British sympathizers; enforce law and order to prevent looting; set up a series of alarm gun warnings; dig earthwork defences; fortify Patterson Park and Federal Hill Park; put 100 cannons into place along Broadway Street and Fayette Street ("The Broadway Barricade" and "The Fayette Street Fortress"); and sink 24 boats and string log and chain booms across Baltimore harbour, with a line of gunboats behind that.

Mary Pickersgill, who lived on Pratt Street in Baltimore, sews two American flags to fly at Fort McHenry, a giant 30 X 42 foot garrison flag, and a smaller 17 X 25 foot storm flag. She starts sewing them in her house, but when they begin to take over the place she moves them to a brewery and finishes them off there. They only take six weeks to make. (Brewing production is altered to make way for the flag sewing, and the brewery also produces a special "Mary Pickersgill Flag Ale" to mark the occasion. To this day in tribute to Mary Pickersgill you'll never find a thirsty Pickersgill in Baltimore).

Artist's depiction of the very last bottle of "Mary Pickersgill Flag Ale" (from description given by the very last "Mary Pickersgill Flag Ale" drinker). Courtesy: Baltimore Flag and Bottle Museum.

The British plan a two-pronged attack on Baltimore. A land attack up the North Point peninsula east of Baltimore (between the Patapsco and Back Rivers), and a water attack directly up the Patapsco River.

At 2:00 a.m. on 12 September 1814 (one day after The Battle of Plattsburgh), the British land 5,000 soldiers and eight cannons in North Point State Park on the south point of the North Point peninsula, 12 miles southeast of Baltimore. The Americans move 3,000 militia out to North Point and set up defences along the narrowest part of the peninsula, at the head of Bear Creek near North Point Village, with a reserve line behind them on the north side of Bread and Cheese Creek. They then issue everybody with peanut butter sandwiches. When the British come into view, advanced American riflemen kill the British general (if you are the only one galloping about on a white horse in a general's uniform acting very generally then you are a pretty good target). The British advance stops while the dead general is taken back to a ship and put in a barrel of rum. The British then move forward again and attack the American line. The Americans are in woods, the British are in a field. After a one hour battle the Americans run (or strategically withdraw) behind Bread and Cheese Creek where everybody is issued with a glass of milk and a slice of Smith Island Cake. The British do not go after them. They camp for the night. It rains. They call it The Battle of North Point (Americans: 24 killed, 139 wounded, 50 prisoners/British: 46 killed, 295 wounded).

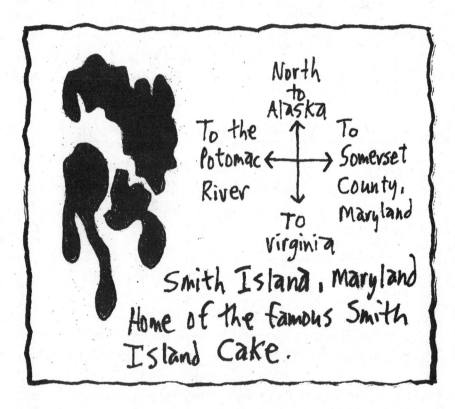

On the morning of 13 September the British land attack continues to advance up the peninsula, through woods, fields, haystacks, creeks, thickets, ponds and swamps, and then stops. They are six miles east of Baltimore. It is 4:15 p.m. It rains.

The British water attack of 11 ships and six bomb/rocket boats, comes up the Patapsco River on 13 September and at 2:00 p.m. begins firing 200 pound shells, rockets with a red glare, and fused bombs that burst in air at Fort McHenry from a distance of two-and-a-half miles (they couldn't get much closer because of the shallow water and the city's harbour defences including Fort McHenry's 57 cannons firing back at them). It rains.

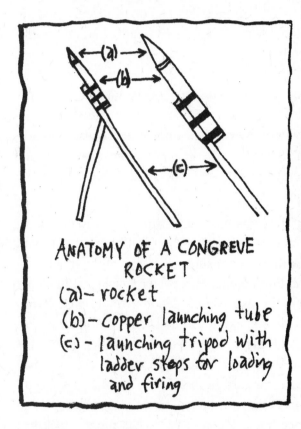

ANATOMY OF A CONGREVE ROCKET
(a) - rocket
(b) - copper launching tube
(c) - launching tripod with ladder steps for loading and firing

The rockets the British fire at Baltimore (and before that at Lacolle, Quebec and Bladensburg and later on at New Orleans) that give such a red glare, are Congreve Rockets invented by Sir William Congreve. They were first tested at The Siege of Boulogne in 1806 when they set the whole town on fire. The rockets are made from a 42-inch-long by four-inch diameter tube of sheet metal filled with gunpowder, that are set off by a fuse and launched from copper tubes mounted on wooden tripods. They turned out to be more terrifying than they were effective however, and were eventually abandoned in 1885.

Held prisoner on board an American ship behind the British fleet is 35-year-old lawyer and amateur poet Francis Scott Key of Georgetown. When the British are returning from the attack on Washington they take as a prisoner Dr. William Beanes of Upper Marlboro, Maryland, a friend of Key's, and Key is one of the two lawyers sent out on an American ship to the British fleet before Baltimore to negotiate his release. From their ship Key witnesses the British firing 1,500-1,800 projectiles at Fort McHenry and its oversized flag during the day and night of 13 September, and in the morning of 14 September "in the dawn's early light," sees that Mary Pickersgill's flag "was still there" despite "the bombs bursting in air" and "the rockets' red glare" (as well as failing to hit the big flag the British only destroy one of Fort McHenry's 57 cannons). On board the ship Key writes a poem that will eventually become the American national anthem. (For more on the life of Francis Scott Key see Appendix: "Francis Scott Key And The American National Anthem.")

On the night of 13 September the British try a new plan, a cleverly coordinated three-pronged attack on Baltimore. The land attack on North Point will launch a surprise, sneak night attack into the city down the North Point Road. The water attack will launch a harbour attack of 1,200 in small boats landing on Locust Point, while at the same time also keeping up the shell, bomb and rocket bombardment of Fort McHenry. At 1:00 a.m. on 14 September the bombardment begins; the harbour attack attacks; and the surprise, sneak night attack sneaks forward in the night. It rains. By 2 a.m. the harbour attack has been stopped and is retreating; the bombardment has stopped; and the surprise, sneak night attack has found that it is not a surprise and is stopped in the vicinity of Patterson Park, Baltimore. But it doesn't stop raining. At 7:00 a.m. the whole attack on Baltimore is called off. The British have fired a bomb a minute at Fort McHenry for the best part of 25 hours, but the only casualties within the fort are four killed, 24 wounded, and the one cannon.

The trajectory of five bombs bursting in air, Mary Pickersgill's flag still there, and the north walls of Fort McHenry from the famous aquatint engraving of The Bombardment of Fort McHenry 1814.

The land attack goes back to its ships, the water attack goes back down the Patapsco River, and the whole Baltimore expedition sails back down Chesapeake Bay; some going to Halifax, Nova Scotia, some to Bermuda, and some to Jamaica. But some of them will be back in December to attack New Orleans in the last major battle of the war.

Thus in the space of 22 days, from 24 August in Washington to 14 September in Baltimore, the British have given the Americans their "White House" and their national anthem (they'd already given them their flag during The American Revolutionary War).

The Ghent, Belgium Peace Talks,
8 August – 24 December 1814

At the same time as the Americans are under siege in Fort Erie and the British are sailing up Chesapeake Bay towards Washington, the two sides have managed to put a team of peace negotiators in the same place (Ghent, Belgium) at the same time (8 August 1814). Now all they have to do is to agree where in Ghent, Belgium to meet at the same place at the same time. The British send a note to the Americans suggesting they meet in the British hotel. The Americans send a note to the British suggesting they meet in the American's hotel. The British send a note to the Americans agreeing to meet in the American's hotel, and they meet there for the first time on 9 August (the Americans have to buy the drinks). There are three British negotiators and five American (although one American missed the first meeting having temporarily left Ghent calling it "this dull hole").

The British present four points for negotiation: Maritime rights, Indian lands, boundaries and fishing rights. The Americans ask for time to consider these and suggest meeting tomorrow in the British hotel. The British agree (and buy the drinks). The meetings will now alternate between the British and American hotels.

On 10 August they discuss Indian lands, write a progress report to their governments, and suspend further meetings until both sides receive instructions. From now on progress at the peace talks will go back and forth depending upon the latest news on the fortunes of the two sides in the war. The Americans lose at Lundy's Lane, Fort Erie, Mackinac, Maine and Washington. The British lose at Plattsburgh and Baltimore.

LONGWOOD HOUSE: Napolean's Prison on St. Helena Island.
The house farthest from any other house and farthest from the sea on the island farthest from any other land in the whole wide world.

As well, the war in Europe still hangs over the British. They are also involved in peace talks about what to do with France.

Despite the fact that France has been defeated and Napoleon exiled to Elba (April 1814), the Duke of Wellington is already becoming uneasy about the possibility of a revival of Napoleon, and the Duke of Wellington carries a lot of influence in determining British policy. His position on the war in North America is that Britain should negotiate a peace treaty there as quickly as possible because the situation in Europe is worrying. He's right. Napoleon escapes from Elba on 1 March 1815, returns to France, raises another army, and begins "The 100 Days" (actually 114 days), that ends with The Battle of Waterloo (18 June, 1815), and Napoleon being captured for the second time (22 June) and being sent far away this time, never to return (the island of St. Helena in the South Atlantic Ocean where he dies on 5 May 1821).

On 19 August the British request a meeting. It lasts one hour and ends with both sides shouting at each other and the British agreeing to put their proposals in writing. They do. By 25 August both sides have agreed that no territory will change hands. By 9 September both sides fear negotiations will break down over the Indian problem, and both sides do not want to be the one that causes negotiations to break down. The British want an Indian state. The Americans don't. The British give in. Then news arrives of the burning of Washington and on 8 October the British issue an "ultimatum" on the Indian situation. The Americans accept the British position. The situation with the Indians will be the same as before the war. The Americans ask to see all the British proposals. The British reply on 22 October. They have no other proposals. All their negotiation points can be negotiated another time. On 31 October they follow this up with another proposal stating that they have no further demands and could the Americans put forward a draft peace treaty.

The British are under pressure to end the war. Just end it. The Duke of Wellington wants it ended. The British parliament wants it ended. The situation in Europe is still not settled. The

Americans are under pressure too. Their economy is in a bad way. Inflation, failing banks, no money for the war, no trade, fewer recruits for the army, and several states have been meeting secretly and could be discussing seceding from The United States. (This is The Hartford Convention of 15 December 1814, in which 26 delegates from Connecticut, Massachusetts, New Hampshire, Rhode Island and Vermont meet for three weeks in Hartford, Connecticut and propose seven amendments to The Untied States Constitution, "Remember The River Raisin" not being one of them).

Hats of The War of 1812.

#8. The Washington "Senators" militia.

The Americans deliver a draft peace treaty to the British on 10 November. Declare peace now, solve problems later, everything to go back to where it was before the war started. The British accept the draft treaty on 27 November. The Americans reply on 30 November and invite the British to meet them on 1 December. The British reply on the same day and propose that they host the meeting (and buy the drinks). They meet on 1 December and 10 December. Then the British bring up boundaries, fishing rights, the Mississippi River and Maine again; and the Americans reject all their proposals.

They meet again on 11 December. The British give in on 22 December. They will sign the draft peace treaty as it is. They meet again on 23 December. The negotiators will sign the treaty, but the war will not be officially over until both governments accept the treaty, and there is a four month deadline for them to do so.

On Christmas Eve 1814 between 4:00 p.m. and 6:00 p.m., the eight negotiators read the 3,294 words contained in the 11 Articles, one Preamble and one Summing Up; and sign six copies of "The Treaty of Peace and Amity, Between His Britannic Majesty and The United States of America" (otherwise known as "The Treaty of Ghent"). Three signed British copies then head for London, and three signed American copies head for Bordeaux, France in order to head for Washington (there are multiple copies in case any get lost).

The treaty basically says that the war is over and both sides are to give back everything taken from the other including places, prisoners, property and papers (Articles 1-3); except islands in the Bay of Fundy, the Maine/New Brunswick boundary, the St. Lawrence River/Great Lakes boundary, and the Lake-of-the-Woods/Lake Superior boundary which are disputed between the two countries and for which future commissions will be set up (Articles 4-8); and that the two sides will end hostilities with the Indians (Article 9); end slavery (Article 10); and have four months to pass the treaty (Article 11).

Over in North America December 1814 has been a busy month too. The British are planning an attack on New Orleans, Louisiana in order to control the Mississippi River, influence the peace negotiations in Ghent, and most importantly, because New Orleans is chock full of two year's worth of trade goods that can't be shipped out and that the British can capture and sell. Booty. Take New Orleans and you take a lot of loot too. The average British soldier can hit the jackpot by taking New Orleans. The peace negotiators in Belgium on the other hand know nothing about the attack on New Orleans (it's underway at the same time as they're signing the treaty). The Americans in New Orleans hardly know anything about it either.

CHAPTER SIX

1815: The Rest of the War of 1812

The Battle of New Orleans, Louisiana, 12 December 1814 – 18 January 1815

The British fleet for the attack on New Orleans leaves Negril Bay, Jamaica on 26 November 1814, with 60 ships, 8,000 soldiers and 40 barges; and by 8 December is moored between Cat Island and Ship Island, Mississippi, 70 miles east of New Orleans. One of their officers is the son of General John Burgoyne who surrendered a whole British army 37 years ago at Saratoga, New York during The American Revolutionary War. Not a good omen.

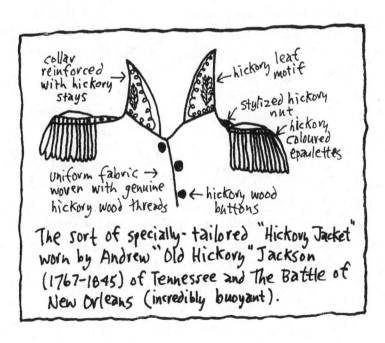

collar reinforced with hickory stays

→ hickory leaf motif

stylized hickory nut

hickory coloured epaulettes

Uniform fabric → woven with genuine hickory wood threads

← hickory wood buttons

The sort of specially-tailored "Hickory Jacket" worn by Andrew "Old Hickory" Jackson (1767-1845) of Tennessee and The Battle of New Orleans (incredibly buoyant).

Louisiana is part of the Seventh Military District with its headquarters at Montgomery, Alabama under the command of Major-General Andrew Jackson of Tennessee, who in 1812 offered to "conquer Quebec in 90 days" with 2,500 Tennessee militia (not a bad idea considering what conquering was done otherwise). The main interest of the Seventh Military District in 1814 though is to take Pensacola, Florida from the Spanish, so because of this they move their headquarters from Montgomery, Alabama to Mobile, Alabama in order to be closer to Pensacola, Florida.

The British had tried to take Fort Morgan at the entrance to Mobile Bay, Alabama on 12 September 1814 with 600 Indians, 130 marines and four ships, but were driven off by the Americans and had gone east along the coast and taken Fort San Carlos at the entrance to Pensacola Bay, Florida instead (vicinity of present-day Pensacola Naval Air Station). On 7 November 1814 the Americans take Pensacola simply by walking in and taking over (the Spanish had abandoned it), and the British then leave Pensacola Bay as well. So when the British fleet is heading for New Orleans the Americans think it is heading to attack Mobile, Alabama again, and it is only when they pass Mobile Bay that the Americans realize it is heading for New Orleans and begin to organize its defence (2 December).

As far as the defence of New Orleans goes, there are three directions the British could attack it from. They could come south down the Mississippi from the north; they could come north up the Mississippi from the south; or they could come west through Mississippi Sound from the east. The Americans think the British will attack from the north. They attack from the east.

The New Orleans Battlefield 1814-15

But New Orleans, Louisiana is a very difficult place to attack no matter what direction you attack it from. From the north is physically the easiest, but you would have to fight your way down the river to get there, past Vicksburg, past Baton Rouge, past lots of places that would try to stop you. Attacking from the south, west or east has less man-made obstacles in the way, but is physically more difficult. You have to get through the Mississippi River delta region. The configuration of the Mississippi delta has changed a lot since 1814, but the substance of it hasn't. It's still a complicated place made up of an irregular shoreline of land mixed together with a maze of islands, bogs, channels, swamps, bayous, ditches, canals, waterlogged woods and mud. Lots of mud (in

1814 too there were sugar cane plantations along a narrow strip on both sides of the river).

New Orleans itself is 100 miles up the Mississippi, with the river, creeks and swamps to the south; creeks and swamps to the west; swamps and Lake Pontchartrain to the north; and the low plains of Chalmette, swamps, sugarcane plantations and Lake Borgne to the east. The British decide to attack from the east, into Lake Borgne and through Chalmette to New Orleans.

The Americans have five gunboats guarding Lake Borgne. On 12 December the British send 45 boats carrying 1,200 soldiers into Lake Borgne, and after "The Battle of Lake Borgne" the Americans have no gunboats left guarding Lake Borgne. The British then begin ferrying troops off the ships between Cat Island and Ship Island, 30 miles west to Pearl River Island, Mississippi at the mouth of the Pearl River (Louisiana-Mississippi border); and from there another 20 miles west across Lake Borgne to the mainland. They then put 1,600 soldiers to work digging a channel five miles farther west from Lake Borgne to the Mississippi River. They're digging in soggy mud. The walls of the channel keep falling in. Swamp reeds are eight feet high. On 21 December they load 2,000 soldiers into boats and begin slogging their way through their channel. The boats get stuck. When they reach solid ground on the other side they make camp on the east shore of the Mississippi River and begin getting ready for Christmas (they draw names, decorate Christmas bulrushes, and everybody goes out Christmas shopping on a regimental rotational basis).

But this attack on New Orleans is taking a lot of time and effort, and is no longer a surprise any more. The Americans know exactly where the British are and where they're going. And on 23 December they spring a surprise, sneak, pre-Christmas night attack on them. They bring a ship down the Mississippi and 2,100 soldiers down from New Orleans, and at 7:30 p.m. on a damp, cloudy evening the ship opens fire on the British camp, and at 9:00 p.m. the soldiers charge into the British camp. Then at midnight the Americans withdraw. They call it "The Christmas Eve Eve Battle". (British: 46 killed, 166 wounded/Americans: 24 killed, 115 wounded).

The next day, Christmas Eve day, the Americans bring a second ship down the Mississippi and bombard the British camp again. Merry Christmas! The real Christmas present though is that The War of 1812 is over and The Battle of New Orleans really doesn't count. But they don't know that yet in Louisiana, so the battle continues.

On Christmas Day in Ghent, Belgium the eight peace negotiators sit down to a Christmas dinner of beef and plum pudding, an orchestra plays the two national anthems ("Yankee Doodle" for the Americans), and toasts are made to the two countries.

Back in Louisiana the British bring in more reinforcements. The Americans withdraw up the river and begin constructing a defensive line 1½ miles long between the British and New Orleans on the Chalmette plantation. The line is behind an empty ditch eight feet deep and 10 feet wide; with swampy woods to the east; the Mississippi River to the west; and an open, harvested sugar cane field in front. The line itself is made up of sugar barrels, earth, and a wood palisade wall; with cannons behind walls made of cotton bales covered with mud. They also put cannons on the west bank of the river and flood the sugar cane field in front just to make it nice and muddy. (The sugar barrels and the cotton bales don't work out so well. The cotton bales catch fire and have to be put out, and the sugar barrels explode when hit sending sugar flying everywhere, clogging up cannons and guns and putting sugar into people's coffee who don't normally take sugar in their coffee).

Both sides now number 4,000. But the British need cannons too, so by Christmas Day they have lugged eight cannons 55 miles from their ships. Merry Christmas! On 27 December the British sink one of the American ships on the Mississippi. On 28 December they attack both ends of the American line and fire off rockets, but the American line and the one remaining ship firing off 800 rounds, stops them. They call it "The Two Days After Boxing Day Battle." The British bring in 16 more cannons. Bigger ones. The Americans reinforce their line and add two more lines behind that.

The British have a new plan for New Orleans. They will blast the American line, charge it, fill in the ditch in one spot so they can get across, while at the same time attacking both ends of the line along the river and in the swampy woods. At 9:00 a.m. on New Year's Eve Day the 16 American cannons and the 24 British cannons open fire on each other. After three hours the American cannons have out-bombarded the British cannons, the British are running out of ammunition, the British attack into the swampy woods has been stopped, and it's starting to rain. The British drag their remaining cannons back out of range, and the Americans repair their line and keep firing at the British. They call it "The New Year's Eve Battle of the Cannons." Happy New Year!

At the same time as the Americans and the British are having a Happy New Year shooting at each other in Louisiana, they're also having a Happy New Year in southern Georgia too. The British Navy has occupied Cumberland Island, Georgia, and on 1 January 1815 they raid St. Marys, Georgia as part of a bigger plan to attack Savannah, Georgia, another American port full of trade goods that can't be shipped out so might as well be captured. (Savannah is a favorite place for the British to attack. They attacked and took Savannah in 1778 during The American Revolutionary War, but they don't get the chance to attack and take it during this war).

On 5 January 1815 the Mayor of Ghent, Belgium holds a banquet to celebrate the signing of the peace treaty, and a band plays "Hail, Columbia" for the Americans and "God Save The King" for the British. The last British peace negotiator leaves Ghent on 7 January, and the last American peace negotiator on 26 January. The furniture used at "The Congress of Ghent" is put up for auction.

The British have another plan for New Orleans. They are becoming bogged down in the bog. They will bring in more reinforcements and attack the Americans on the west bank of the river, along the east bank of the river, and in the defensive line (except this time with ladders to scale the ditch and walls). They will also bring the navy up the Mississippi, and enlarge an existing canal to allow bigger boats to get from Lake Borgne to the Mississippi. The attack on New Orleans is turning into a major civil engineering work. And they still haven't even reached the city yet. It's a very intricate plan. Too intricate.

Hats of The War of 1812.

#9. The New Orleans "Saints" Militia.

By 7 January the British have 42 boats ready to go into the canal, and 5,800 soldiers ready to attack: 2,200 for the frontal attack, 1,200 for the west bank attack, 1,200 for the east bank attack, and 1,200 in reserve. The Americans have 8,800 defenders including the well known but seldom seen Haitian pirate Jean Lafitte, or Laffite, who keeps the spelling of his last name as much of a mystery as he keeps his whereabouts, hiding out in the Grand Terre Islands and Barataria Bay along the Gulf coast; and who has for his participation in The Battle of New Orleans on behalf of the

Americans (the British wanted him too), two towns and an historical park named after him.

← jaunty pirate hat with feather
← pirate curls
← patch over left eye
← scar on cheek
← jaunty pirate mustache and goatee
bloodshot good eye →
gold ear-ring (hidden) →

One of the many drawings trying to portray the likeness of the famous pirate Jean Laffite/Lafitte. No authenticated likeness exists.

At 4:00 a.m. on the morning of 8 January 1815, the British launch their final attack of The Battle of New Orleans, and the last major attack of The War of 1812. They wished they hadn't. The Americans are waiting for them. The British march across the open, harvested, muddy, sugar cane field in the early morning mist. Then the mist rises. They're sitting ducks. The British commander is killed. The reserves go in. They fail to cross the ditch. After 30 minutes they retreat. It's The Battle of Bunker Hill all over again, except without the hill. Defenceless soldiers marching out in the open against a heavily defended position. It's not a pretty sight for the British. It's an absolute total failure.

The canal attack is also having trouble. The canal is not deep enough for some of the boats. The walls collapse. Boats have to be pushed. Some boats reach the Mississippi, but are carried down river by the strong current. More failure. The east bank attack forgets their ladders and has to go back and get them. They are stopped and also retreat. More failure.

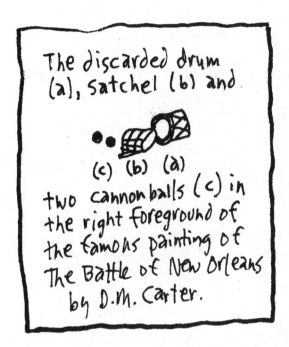

The discarded drum (a), satchel (b) and

(c) (b) (a)

two cannon balls (c) in the right foreground of the famous painting of The Battle of New Orleans by D.M. Carter.

The west bank attack presses forward and captures an American cannon with the inscription on it: "Taken at the Surrender of Yorktown 1781." Another bad omen. But they have no support and so they too retreat. More failure. It rains. The British withdraw. Some of their heavy cannons sink in the mud and have to be abandoned. Both sides wait. On 9 January they agree to a cease-fire to bury their dead. In the mud. Then the Americans continue bombarding the British. It rains. It's cold and damp and miserable. The Mississippi floods. British soldiers desert. It's all a terrible, dismal failure for the British.

The British Navy comes 30 miles up the Mississippi and fires at a fort that is no longer there from 9-17 January, but gets no farther and leaves on 18 January. That same day the Americans and the British exchange prisoners, and that night the British begin secretly retreating back to their ships. They build nine miles of temporary roads and 16 bridges through swamps and over creeks so that they can get out a different way than they came in. It takes nine days.

The Americans come out from behind their line to go and have a peek at the British camp to see what is going on, and find it deserted except for 3,000 abandoned cannonballs and 80 wounded British soldiers; and on 21 January they march triumphantly the five miles north into New Orleans to celebrate

Part of the label, including the hole, of a 45 r.p.m. recording of "The Battle of New Orleans" by Johnny Horton, April 1959.

JOHNNY HORTON

2:28

THE BATTLE OF NEW ORLEANS
~ ARR: JIMMIE DRIFTWOOD ~

their victory. The Americans snipe at the British now and again as they are leaving, but they don't attack them again. The Battle of New Orleans is over. It's the biggest battle of The War of 1812 and a terribly one-sided British defeat later commemorated by Jimmie Driftwood's stirring but somewhat historically inaccurate 1959 ballad "*The Battle of New Orleans*" (also recorded by Lonnie Donegan and Johnny Horton. The British don't "run down the Mississippi to the Gulf of Mexico," they slowly slip away to the east the way they'd come in). Three of the four British generals involved at New Orleans are killed. British: 850 killed, 2,400 wounded/American: 55 killed, 185 wounded/total 3,490 (Lundy's Lane 1,737).

The New Orleans battle field today at Chalmette, Louisiana is partly lost under the Mississippi River. "The Battle of New Orleans" should probably be called "The Battle of Chalmette."

Chalmette was as far as the British army got. They never got to New Orleans. But because there wasn't much at Chalmette in 1815, it was only one of a number of plantations along the east bank of the Mississippi; and because New Orleans was bigger and better known than Chalmette; and because New Orleans was where the British were heading for, not Chalmette; and because New Orleans is much more fun to say and sing about than Chalmette, it became known as "The Battle of New Orleans" not "The Battle of Chalmette."

The End of The War of 1812

The British retreat from New Orleans takes until 28 January 1815. Then a storm comes up keeping them in Mississippi Sound until 6 February when they sail east to Dauphin Island, Alabama on the west side of the entrance to Mobile Bay across from Fort Morgan that they'd tried to take in 1814. Fort Morgan is defended by 370 American soldiers, 22 cannons and 16 women and children. On 8 February the British land 1,000 soldiers east of the fort, set up 16 cannons pointing at the fort, and on 11 February ask Fort Morgan to surrender, which it does on 12 February. The Americans meanwhile have sent 1,000 soldiers south from Mobile, Alabama to reinforce Fort Morgan (11 February). They land near Gasque, Alabama east of Fort Morgan just as Fort Morgan is surrendering. Then, as British ships are now entering Mobile Bay, the American ships quickly sail back to Mobile leaving the soldiers on the peninsula to hike it back to Mobile themselves along the east side of Mobile Bay.

The diplomatic part of The War of 1812 ends officially when The United States government passes The Treaty of Ghent on 17 February 1815 (the British parliament passed it on 28 December 1814).

The fighting part of The War of 1812 ends when a British ship arrives in Mobile Bay on 13 February 1815 with news that

The Treaty of Ghent had been signed 50 days ago. The British remain on Dauphin Island with its mosquitoes, sand flies, snakes and alligators until 5 March when they hear that the war is officially over. They then sail for Europe and back to war again against Napoleon.

Andrew Jackson goes on to become president of The United States and have his statue put in a square named after him in New Orleans. Jean Lafitte, or Laffite, returns to being a pirate; relocates to Galveston Island, Texas; retires to St. Louis, Missouri; and dies in Alton, Illinois in 1854. News of the peace treaty doesn't reach Quebec City, Canada, now virtually forgotten in the war, until 1 March 1815. As a result of this Lord George Prevost sets off from Quebec City in the winter to go to Britain for his court-martial. He travels overland from Quebec to Halifax, Nova Scotia and from Halifax to Britain by ship, but dies 11 days before the court-martial begins, age 49, mainly as a result of the exertions of the trip.

Hats of The
War of 1812.

#10. The Buffalo,
New York Niagara
Aquatic Militia.

CHAPTER SEVEN

After the War of 1812

Slowly and gradually the two sides begin fulfilling the terms of The Treaty of Ghent. The British leave Mackinac Island and Fort Niagara, and the Americans leave Amherstburg in July 1815. But the British don't leave Eastport, Maine until June 1818; and Astoria, Oregon until 1842, the same year the Maine/New Brunswick boundary is finally settled. The Lake-of-the-Woods/Lake Superior boundary isn't settled until 1875.

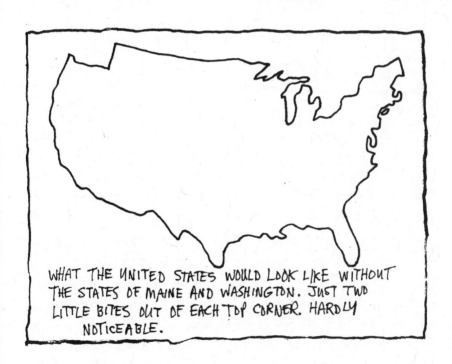

WHAT THE UNITED STATES WOULD LOOK LIKE WITHOUT THE STATES OF MAINE AND WASHINGTON. JUST TWO LITTLE BITES OUT OF EACH TOP CORNER. HARDLY NOTICEABLE.

The war may be over but the two sides really do not trust each other for some time afterwards (especially the Canadians), and they begin constructing military works in case of being attacked again (or wanting to attack). The Americans build roads to better connect Sackets Harbor and Plattsburgh with the rest of the country; and James Monroe, the Secretary of War, has a plan for an invasion of Canada in 1815 involving a regular army and 30,000 militia attacking across the St. Lawrence River between Kingston and Montreal (they should have thought about that one in 1812, no wonder the Canadians are so nervous).

Favourite War of 1812 Aperitifs

Canada builds Fort Henry at Kingston, the Rideau Canal between Kingston and Ottawa, a new naval base at Penetanguishene, Ontario on Georgian Bay with a connecting road from Lake Simcoe, and upgrades the defences of Halifax and Quebec City; all because of this nervousness about what the Americans might do.

Despite the last battle of The War of 1812 being fought at New Orleans (second last at Fort Erie), The War of 1812 was started by The United States for the specific purpose of conquering Canada. That they failed to do so was due to the defence of the country by the British, and, as the Duke of Wellington put it, because of "the inexperience of the officers of The United States in the operations of the war."

As a result of The War of 1812, The United States grows south and west, not north; four future American presidents base their popularity on their war experience (Monroe, Adams, Jackson, Harrison); and The United States finally recognizes the benefits of having a regular army instead of relying too heavily on part-time militia (they could have learned this lesson after The American Revolutionary War too).

The War of 1812 is quickly forgotten in Britain. On 1 March 1815 Napoleon escapes and the war with France is back on again until 18 June 1815 when Napoleon is finally defeated once and for all at The Battle of Waterloo.

The War of 1812 is remembered in Canada, but not as much as it should be.

The War of 1812 is remembered in The United States, but only for the good bits, and only in those places that participated in it.

The Holland Landing Anchor. En route from Britain to Georgian Bay during The War of 1812, it is abandoned at Holland Landing, Ontario when the war is over. It's still there.

The Napoleonic Wars and The War of 1812 both happened at the same time. One was a great long war; and the other was a small short war. But when they ended they both had the same result. The Napoleonic Wars ended any chance of the domination of Europe by France. And The War of 1812 ended any chance of the domination of North America by The United States.

The War of 1812 may be a small, little known and under-appreciated war. But it had quite a big influence over the development of the world's third largest continent.

Hats of The War of 1812.

#11. The Amherstburg, Ontario Toque Brigade.

APPENDIX

Laura Secord After the War of 1812

The sort of white cotton bonnet Laura Secord is still wearing late in life (with accompanying scarf).

I ♥ Beaver Dams

After The War of 1812 ended, Laura and James Secord of Queenston, Ontario petition the government for compensation for war wounds and loss of livelihood. They obtain a lease on a stone quarry, James is appointed a Court Registrar (it sounds better than it pays), and Laura is promised the job of caretaker of Brock's Monument, but doesn't get it. She also starts writing to Captain James FitzGibbon seeking his help in supporting her petitions to the government for assistance.

Fifteen years after the war ends, Laura Secord writes a letter to her sister: "I am sorry to say that we are not very prosperous." They never are. In 1833 James is promoted to Judge (it sounds better than it pays). Two years later he resigns to become The Collector of Customs at Chippawa, Ontario (south of Niagara Falls). They move to Chippawa. Five years later they petition the government for the Queenston ferry concession. In this petition Laura quotes from a certificate written on her behalf by Captain FitzGibbon. It doesn't help. They don't get this job either.

In 1841 James Secord dies. Laura Secord is a 65-year-old widow with three widowed daughters, grandchildren, and no money. Her husband's pension is stopped. She is back petitioning the government again.

Laura (Ingersoll) Secord was born in Great Barrington, Massachusetts, USA in 1775, and came to Canada in 1793 age 18, when her father, who fought for the Americans in The American Revolutionary War, came to Canada for a grant of free land along the Thames River in Oxford County, Ontario. By this time Laura and her three sisters had already had three mothers. The first died when Laura was eight, and seven years later they were on their third. At age 15 Laura was described as being "delicate and frail."

Two years after coming to Canada (1795), the Ingersoll family move to Queenston, Ontario where her father operates a tavern. Two years after that Laura Ingersoll marries James Secord. When the Ingersoll family moves back again to Oxford County to found the present-day town of Ingersoll, Ontario (west of Woodstock, Ontario), Laura stays behind in Queenston to become the wife of a struggling merchant and a belated hero of The War of 1812.

When the Americans cross the Niagara River and attack Queenston on 13 October 1812, the village has a population of 300 including Laura and James Secord and their five children. Laura leads the children out of the village to a farm a mile away, and Sergeant James Secord goes off to fight in The Battle of Queenston Heights. In the middle of that afternoon Laura walks back into Queenston to see what has happened, and learns that James has been wounded in Brock's charge up the heights and has not returned. She goes looking for him and finds him on the hill with a bullet in his knee and a wounded shoulder. She takes him home, nurses him back to health, and probably saves his life. But from then on James Secord has a bad knee.

After her husband dies Laura Secord buys a house in Chippawa (this is now the second Laura Secord House), and the Ingersoll family lands near Ingersoll, Ontario are sold. It is not until 1845, 31 years after The War of 1812 ended, that the first published accounts of Laura Secord's deeds during the war appear. This only happens because James FirtGibbon is about to be rewarded with 5,000 acres of land for his "war services," and Laura Secord's son Charles challenges this grant citing a certificate written by FitzGibbon mentioning Laura Secord's part in The Battle of Beaver Dams. But not much attention is paid to Laura Secord.

A book about the war is published in 1853, and Laura herself writes a section in it. But not much attention is paid to Laura Secord.

By 1860 Laura Secord is 85 years old. That year a 19-year-old Prince Albert Edward, Prince of Wales (the future King Edward VII), visits Niagara Falls and attends a ceremony at Brock's Monument. The Falls are illuminated for the first time. They are impressive. But the young prince is even more impressed by the fact that there is only one woman's name on the list of War of 1812 war veterans. He sends Laura Secord £150 in gold.

A newspaper follows up on the story of why The Prince of Wales would send an old lady in Canada £150 in gold. The first book on Laura Secord is published in 1864. Fifty-one years after walking 19 miles to help save Canada from invasion by The United States, Laura Secord is finally recognized as a hero. Four years later she dies on 17 October 1868, age 93. Poor and still relatively forgotten.

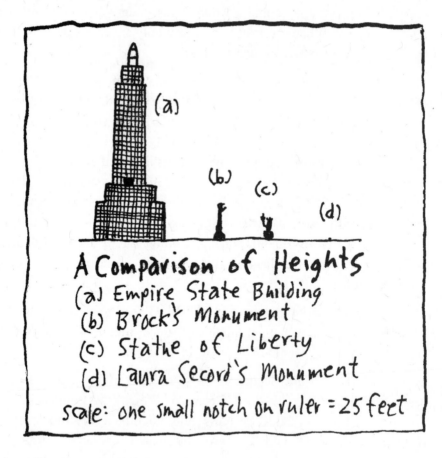

A Comparison of Heights
(a) Empire State Building
(b) Brock's Monument
(c) Statue of Liberty
(d) Laura Secord's Monument
Scale: one small notch on ruler = 25 feet

Other books on Laura Secord follow in 1869, 1887, 1889, 1891 and 1900. After the 1891 book a memorial stone is erected at her grave site in Chippawa. It reads:

*"To perpetuate the Name and Fame of
Laura Secord who walked alone nearly
20 miles by a circuitous, difficult and
perilous route, through woods and
swamps, and over miry roads to warn a
British outpost at DeCew's Falls of an
intended attack, and thereby enabled
Lieut. FitzGibbon on the 24 June 1813
with less than fifty men of H.M. 49th
Regiment, about 15 militia men and a
small force of Six Nation and other
Indians under Captain William Johnson
Kerr and Dominique Ducharme, to
surprise and attack the enemy at Beek
Woods (or Beaver Dams), and after a
short engagement to capture Col.
Boerstler of the US. Army and his entire
force of 542 men with two field pieces."*

The proceeds from the 1900 book pays to erect a 12-foot-high monument on Queenston Heights in 1910 near General Brock's 210-foot tower. It reads:

*"To Laura Secord who saved her
husband's life in the Battle of
Queenston Heights, 13 October 1812,
and who risked her own in conveying to
Captain FitzGibbon information by
which he won the victory of Beaver
Dams."*

In 1905 a painting of Laura Secord is commissioned and hung in the Ontario Parliament buildings in Toronto. In 1913 the Laura Secord candy shops are founded (later ice cream, chocolates and candy). They are still in business today. But it is 100 years too late to benefit the real Laura Secord.

A Chocolate Similar To The Type Named After Laura Secord. (hard outside, soft inside)

In 1914 a Memorial Hall is built as part of the Laura Secord School in Queenston. But by 1930 a history book is written for the Province of Ontario which fails to mention her. Laura Secord is beginning to be forgotten by history again.

It is not until 1959 that a certificate written by James Fitzgibbon in support of Laura Secord is discovered in the Public Archives of Canada in Ottawa. It is dated 11 May 1827, and it is the second of three written accounts sent by FitzGibbon to the Canadian government verifying the events of Laura Secord's walk on 22 June 1813. FitzGibbon had been writing to the government as Laura Secord had asked him to, but Laura Secord had been lost and buried by government bureaucracy. The other two certificates are dated 1820 and 1837. They are the only written accounts that confirm what Laura Secord did on a hot, humid June day in 1813 to try and help her country.

Francis Scott Key and the American National Anthem

Francis Scott Key was not a professional national anthem writer. He was a lawyer who liked to write poetry in his spare time. In 1814 Key was 35 years old, married with children, and living in Georgetown near Washington D.C. When the British are advancing on Washington, Key sends his wife to Middlebrook, Maryland; takes his children to Frederick, Maryland; hires two wagons to go back to Georgetown and remove the possessions from his house; and returns to Georgetown himself. Key is then one of those who goes out to watch The Battle of Bladensburg as a non-participating spectator (he goes with a militia commander).

When the British return to Upper Marlboro, Maryland after having burned Washington, they take as a prisoner Dr. William Beanes, a friend of Francis Scott Key's, who is still in Upper Marlboro having been there when the British first marched through on their way to Bladensburg. Beanes is held for "hostile conduct" against the British. The British put Dr. Beanes on a ship and take him down the Patuxent River and away from Washington, and then up Chesapeake Bay and up the Patapsco River towards Baltimore. Before the British Navy attacks Baltimore the Americans send two lawyers out on a ship to the British fleet to negotiate the release of Dr. Beanes, and one of these two lawyers is Francis Scott Key (7 September).

And so Key, who was born near Keymar in a quiet, rural corner of northern Maryland and had practiced law in nearby Frederick, Maryland, is pitched headfirst into The War of 1812. He is one of those kept prisoner on board the American ship who witnesses the bombardment of Baltimore from the viewpoint of the river behind the British fleet. And so he sees "the bombs bursting in air," and "the rockets' red glare," and that Mary Pickersgill's "flag was still there" flying over Fort McHenry "in the dawn's early light;" from a vantage point that not many other Americans had (certainly none that wrote poetry).

Key makes his first notes on a poem about Fort McHenry on the back of a letter he had in his pocket while on board the ship, and by the time the British release the American ship on 16 September (Dr. Beanes is released on evidence that he assisted wounded British soldiers after The Battle of Bladensburg), the poem is complete: 32 lines in four stanzas of eight lines each. As yet it has no title.

An American Artillery Caisson (Wagon) 1814 Model – Star of the future hit U.S. Army Anthem: "And The Caissons Go Rolling Along" by Major Edward L. Gruber 1907. "Over hill over dale, As we hit the dusty trail, And the caissons go rolling along."

After his release Key stays in a Baltimore hotel and writes out the poem again under the title *The Defence of Fort McHenry*. The poem is printed on a handbill and circulated in Baltimore on 17 September, and is first published anonymously in a Baltimore newspaper on 21 September 1814. So the words part of the American national anthem are complete.

The music part of the American national anthem was written by John Stafford Smith (1750-1836), a British musician, conductor, composer and organist; as the music to the words of *To Anacreon in Heaven*, which became the official song of The Anacreontic Society of London, U.K., a social-musical-masonic organization that lasted from 1771-1794. Anacreon was a Greek writer of love poems and drinking songs. There was a Columbian Anacreontic Society in New York City in 1795 that would have also sung this song, so the song was in The United States well before 1814.

Somewhere along the line Francis Scott Key hears the Anacreon song, likes it, puts his poem to the tune of this song, and changes the title of his poem and song from *The Defence of Fort McHenry* to *The Star-Spangled Banner*. Over time as well the words and music to the song both changed somewhat, but the basis of Key's words and Smith's music still remain in *The Star-Spangled Banner* as it is sung and played today.

The song becomes popular and is adopted by the American Army and Navy, but unfortunately all the really good things that happened to *The Star-Spangled Banner* happen after Francis Scott Key dies in 1843 (age 64). The poem is published in a book entitled *Poems of the Late Francis S. Key Esq.* in 1857, and the song is adopted as the American national anthem in 1931.

After The War of 1812 is over Francis Scott Key is sent by President Andrew Jackson to settle an Indian land dispute in Alabama (1833), helps found "The American Colonization Society" which tries to end slavery by sending slaves back to Africa, and becomes the District Attorney of the District of Columbia (1833-1841). But he never has as much excitement again as he had that night on board a ship in the Patapsco River south of Baltimore in September 1814, that inspired him to write his famous poem.

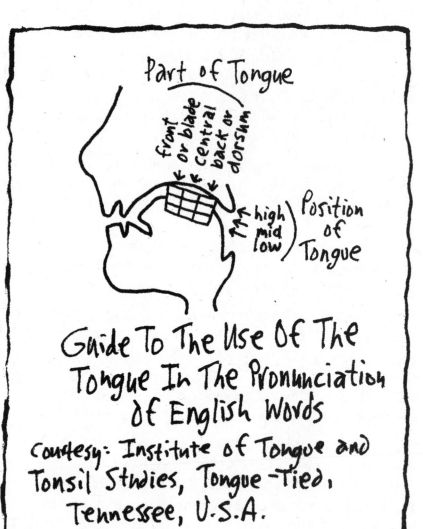

Guide To The Use Of The Tongue In The Pronunciation Of English Words

Courtesy: Institute of Tongue and Tonsil Studies, Tongue-Tied, Tennessee, U.S.A.

APPENDIX

Fun Words to Say from the War of 1812

(With A Spelling and Pronunciation Guide)

Chateauguay	(4)	– Shatow-*gay*
Detroit	(3)	– Dee-*troyt* or *Dee*-troyt or Dee-troy-*at* or Motown
Fort Meigs		– Fort Megs
Gananoque	(4)	– Gan-an-*awk*-kway
Lake Borgne		– Lake Born
Lake Pontchartrain		– Pon-shar-*train* (Lake Pontchartrain did not feature in The Battle of New Orleans or The War of 1812, but it's included here because it's such a lovely name and much more fun to say than Lake Borgne. It also has a beautiful folk song written about it called *The Lakes of Pontchartrain*).
Lundy's Lane		– Lundy's Lane
Maumee River		– *Maw*-me, *maw*-me, how I love you, how I love you, my dear old *Maw*-me
New Orleans	(3)	– New Or-*leens* or New Or-*luns* or New Or-*lins* or New *Or*-lee-ans

Oswego		– Osh-*wee*-go (off-we-go to Osh-*wee*-go)
Patapsco River		– Pa-*tap*-sco
Patuxent River		– Pa-tux-*ent*
Passamaquoddy Bay	(1)	– Pass-a-maw-*kwaw*-dee
Penobscot	(2)	– Pen-*ob*-scot
Potomac River		– Poe-*tow*-mick
Prairie due Chien		– Prairie Dog or Prairie-dew-*shen*
Richelieu River	(4)	– Rish-el-*loo*

(1) Denotes winner of "The Most Fun Place To Say In The War of 1812 Award."

(2) Denotes runner-up in "The Most Fun Place To Say In The War Of 1812 Award."

(3) Denotes winner of "The Most Difficult Place To Say In The War Of 1812 Award" (joint winners).

(4) Denotes winner of "The Most Difficult Place To Spell In The War Of 1812 Award" (joint winners).

WEAPONS OF THE WAR OF 1812

American "Springfield" Musket

British "India Pattern" Musket

American Militia "Wooden Training" Musket

Indian Combination Paddle and Tomahawk Musket

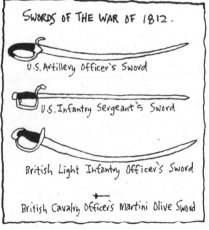

SWORDS OF THE WAR OF 1812.

U.S. Artillery Officer's Sword

U.S. Infantry Sergeant's Sword

British Light Infantry Officer's Sword

British Cavalry Officer's Martini Olive Sword

A Guide To War of 1812 Fort Terminology

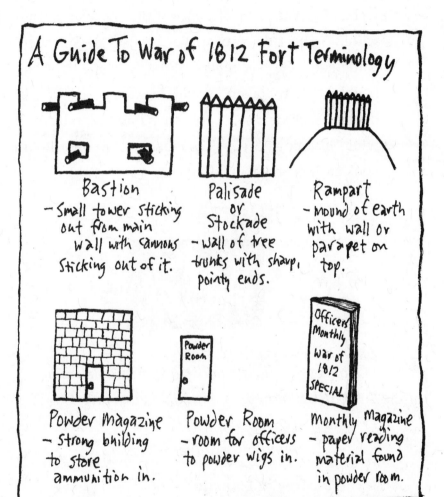

Bastion
- Small tower sticking out from main wall with cannons sticking out of it.

Palisade or Stockade
- Wall of tree trunks with sharp, pointy ends.

Rampart
- mound of earth with wall or parapet on top.

Powder Magazine
- Strong building to store ammunition in.

Powder Room
- room for officers to powder wigs in.

Powder Room

Monthly Magazine
- paper reading material found in powder room.

Officers Monthly War of 1812 SPECIAL

About the Author

Geoffrey Corfield lives in Canada. In fact he was born here. He lives within a bicycle ride, or a brisk walk, of a War of 1812 historical site and plaque; and within a short drive of a War of 1812 re-enactment battle site. He has climbed Brock's Monument and had his photo taken beside Laura Secord's. His hobbies include used book shops and sipping port while listening to classical music. This is his sixth book and second about a war.

Illustrations by

Geoffrey Corfield's books are available from DESPUB at $14.95 to $16.95 each plus G.S.T. (5%) and are shipped with no charge for shipping, handling or other gimmicks.

Toll-free in Canada 1-866-471-4123

email: despub@gmail.com